THE CREATION OF THE WORLD

or

Globalization

SUNY SERIES IN CONTEMPORARY FRENCH THOUGHT

David Pettigrew and François Raffoul, editors

Jean-Luc Nancy

THE CREATION OF THE WORLD

or

Globalization

Translated and with an Introduction by
François Raffoul and David Pettigrew

STATE UNIVERSITY OF NEW YORK PRESS

Published by
STATE UNIVERSITY OF NEW YORK PRESS
ALBANY

© 2007 State University of New York

For information, contact State University of New York Press, Albany, NY
www.sunypress.edu

Production, Laurie Searl
Marketing, Anne M. Valentine

Library of Congress Cataloging-in-Publication Data

Nancy, Jean-Luc.
   [La création du monde ou la mondialisation. English]
   The creation of the world or globalization / Jean-Luc Nancy ; translated and introduction by François Raffoul, David Pettigrew.
      p. cm. — (Suny series in contemporary French thought)
   Includes bibliographical references and index.
   ISBN-13: 978-0-7914-7025-1 (hardcover : alk. paper)
   ISBN-13: 978-0-7914-7026-8 (pbk. : alk. paper)
   1. Globalization—Philosophy. 2. Political science—Philosophy. 3. Teleology. I. Title.

B2430.N363C7413 2007
303.48'201—dc22

                                                                          2006013428

10   9   8   7   6   5   4   3   2   1

Contents

Translators' Acknowledgments

We would like to thank Jane Bunker, editor-in-chief of SUNY Press, for her support of this project from its earliest stages.

We also would like to express our appreciation for the support provided by a Connecticut State University Research Grant and for the research-reassigned time provided by DonnaJean Fredeen, Dean of the School of Arts and Sciences of Southern Connecticut State University (SCSU). We also thank J. Philip Smith, former Interim President, and Ellen Beatty, Associate Vice President for Academic Affairs, of SCSU for their support of the translation project from its inception. Thanks to Troy Paddock, Associate Professor of History at SCSU, for his assistance with our research regarding Carl Schmitt.

At Louisiana State University, we are especially grateful to John Castore for his assistance with the preface, and to Troy Mellon for her careful review of the final manuscript.

We thank Cathy Leblanc, Professor of English at the *Université de Lille 3*, as well as Pierre Jacerme, Professor Emeritus of *Lettres Supérieures* at lycée Henri IV for their advice concerning key translation questions.

For all of her support our appreciation goes to Mélida Badilla Carmona.

Finally, we would like to express our gratitude to Professor Jean-Luc Nancy for his generosity and help concerning the translation.

Translators' Introduction

I

The thinking of the world developed in *The Creation of the World* or *Globalization*[1] unfolds in a play between two terms that are apparently synonymous, or used interchangeably, namely, *globalisation* and *mondialisation*. Nancy addresses, in his prefatory note to the English edition of the text, this linguistic particularity found in the French language, which possesses two terms for designating the phenomenon known in English simply as "globalization"; these terms, *globalisation* and *mondialisation*, are rendered here as globalization and world-forming, respectively. As a matter of fact, the term *globalization*, as Nancy notes, "has already established itself in the areas of the world that use English for contemporary information exchange" (CW, 27), whereas "*mondialisation*" does not allow itself to be translated as easily and would even be, according to Nancy, untranslatable. If the two terms seem, at first glance, to be indistinguishable, converging in the designation of the same phenomenon, that is, the unification of all parts of the world, in fact they reveal two quite distinct, if not opposite, meanings. At stake in this distinction is nothing less than two possible destinies of our humanity, of our time. On the one hand, there is the uniformity produced by a global economical and technological logic—Nancy specifies, "a global injustice against the background of general equivalence" (CW, 54)—leading toward the opposite of an inhabitable world, to "the un-world" [*immonde*]. And, on the other hand, there is the possibility of an authentic *world-forming*, that is, of a making of the world and of a making sense that Nancy will call, for reasons we will clarify later, a "creation" of the world. This creation of the world means, as he makes clear, "immediately, without delay, reopening each possible struggle for a world, that is, for what must form the contrary" of globality (ibid.).[2]

It is this contrast in meaning that Nancy endeavors to reveal in order to open the possibility of a world. From the beginning, he emphasizes that the global or globality is a phenomenon that is more abstract than the worldly or world-forming; he refers to globality as a "totality grasped as a whole," an "indistinct totality," while the world, the worldly, world-forming calls to mind rather a "process in expansion," in reference to the world of humans, of culture, and of nations in a differentiated set. In the final analysis, what interests Nancy, in this distinction between "world-forming" and "globalization," is that world-forming maintains a crucial reference to the world's horizon, as a space of human relations, as a space of meaning held in common, a space of significations or of possible significance. On the other hand, globalization is a process that indicates an "enclosure in the undifferentiated sphere of a unitotality" (CW, 28) that is perfectly accessible and transparent for a mastery without remainder. Therefore, it is not insignificant that the term *mondialisation* remains untranslatable, while globalization tends to the integral translatability of all meanings and all phenomena. Nancy will therefore have a tendency to oppose these two terms, to mark their contrast, going as far as to suggest that globalization, far from being a becoming-world, would lead, rather, to a proliferation of the un-world. At the beginning of the book, Nancy questions whether the phenomenon of globalization leads to the giving birth of a world or to its contrary. Further, within the essay "*Urbi et orbi*" he discusses globalization as "the suppression of all world-forming of the world," as "an unprecedented geopolitical, economic, and ecological catastrophe" (CW, 50). The question, henceforth, becomes the following: "How are we to conceive of, precisely, a world where we only find a globe, an astral universe, or an earth without sky . . . ?" (CW, 47).

Nancy begins with the following fact: the world destroys itself. Here it is not a matter, he clarifies, of hyperbole, fear, or anxiety, or something catastrophic; or of a hypothesis for reflection. No, it is, according to Nancy, a fact, indeed *the* fact from which his reflection originates. "The fact that the world is destroying itself is not a hypothesis: it is, in a sense, the fact from which any thinking of the world follows" (CW, 35). The thought of the world, of the being-world of the world, is thus rendered possible, paradoxically, when the world destroys itself or is in the process of destroying itself. In effect, it is "thanks to" the event of globalization—for Nancy, the suppression of the world—that the world is in the position to appear *as such*. Globalization destroys the world and thus makes possible the emergence of the question relating to its being. This is why Nancy begins his thought of the world with an analysis of globalization, that is, the destruction of the world.

Noting briefly the features of this destruction, Nancy highlights the shift in meaning of the papal formulation "*urbi et orbi*," which has come to mean, in

2

ordinary language, "everywhere and anywhere." This "everywhere and any-where" consecrates the disintegration of the world, because it is no longer pos-sible, since this disintegration, to form an orb of the world. The orb of the world dissolves in the non-place of global multiplicity. This is an extension that leads to the indistinctness of the parts of the world, as for instance, the urban in relation to the rural. Nancy calls this hyperbolic accumulation "agglomeration," in the sense of the conglomerate, of the piling up, of which the "bad infinite" (CW, 47) dismantles the world:[3]

> This network cast upon the planet—and already around it, in the orbital band of satellites along with their debris—deforms the *orbis* as much as the *urbs*. The agglomeration invades and erodes what used to be thought of as *globe* and which is nothing more now than its double, *glomus*. In such a *glomus*, we see the conjunction of an indefinite growth of techno-science, of a correla-tive exponential growth of populations, of a worsening of inequalities of all sorts within these populations—economic, biological and cultural—and of a dissipation of the certainties, images and identities of what the world was with its parts and humanity with its characteristics. (CW, 33–34)

The accumulation of globalization is a concentration of wealth that never occurs without the exclusion of a margin that is rejected into misery. Nancy thus notes the correlation of the process of technological and economic plan-etary domination with the disintegration of the world, that is, the disintegra-tion of the "convergence of knowledge, ethics, and social well-being" (CW, 34). Everything happens as if accessing the planetary, the covering of the world in all its totality, made the world at the same time disappear, as the meaning of the totalizing movement also disappears. The access to totality, in the sense of the global and of the planetary, is at the same time the disappearing of the world. It is also, Nancy emphasizes, the end of the orientation and of the sense (of the world). Globality does not open a path, a way, or a direction, a possi-bility; rather, it furiously turns on itself and exacerbates itself as the blind tech-nological and economical exploitation, on its absence of perspective and ori-entation. In short, "The world has lost its capacity to form a world [*faire monde*]" (ibid.). The profound nihilism of the logic of globalization is here revealed for, as Nancy concludes, "everything takes place as if the world affected and permeated itself with a death drive that soon would have noth-ing else to destroy than the world itself" (ibid.).

Thus, what appears in this too brief recapitulation is, on the one hand, the antinomy between the global and the worldly (which allows for a differentiat-ing of the thought of world-forming in opposition to globalization), but also,

3

above all, the role that the appearance of the nothing that plays in the world, in its event as in its destruction or in its destruction as event.[4] It is therefore a question for us of bringing forth this "nothing of the world," whose characteristics Nancy reveals, for one senses that it is in this nothing that the cross-destinies of globalization and world-forming are at stake, as well as the question of contemporary nihilism; a nihilism whose hard knot will have been fractured by the nothing of the *ex nihilo* of the creation of the world.

At first, Nancy begins to reconstruct the historic emergence of the question of the world, that is, the way in which the world is becoming a proper philosophical question, through a process that he calls the "becoming-world of the world" (CW, 41). The world as problem and as the proper site of human existence was covered, obscured, by the classical figures of onto-theology and representational thinking, all the while, paradoxically and silently, undermining onto-theology from within. The world, writes Nancy in a striking passage, was or has formed "the self-deconstruction that undermines from within onto-theology." (ibid.).

Nancy begins by noting that the world emerges as world when it comes out of representation,[5] when it frees itself of the so-called worldview or *Weltanschauung*. The representation of the world, in effect, implies a vantage point, therefore a position that is outside of the world, from where the world may be able to be seen and represented. Such a representation reduces and, thus, neutralizes the world. This is why Nancy insists on the fact that the world emerges as world against the background of a historical withdrawal of the representation of the world. Such a representation supposes a *cosmotheoros*, that is to say, a subject-of-the-world representing the world in front of itself as an object. It supposes, on the other hand, the representation of a principle and of an end of the world, the world ending in such a view; it devotes itself, in the end, to the reduction of the world to the status of an object, a world regarded as "objective." However, it is from all these features that the world escapes: "The world is no longer conceived of as a representation. . . . The world is thus outside representation, outside its representation and of a world of representation, and this is how, no doubt, one reaches the most contemporary determination of the world" (CW, 43). A *subject-of-the-world* keeps the world in its gaze, its sight, in such a way that the world is thus represented as "a world dependent on the gaze of a subject-of-the-world" (CW, 40). As for this subject, it is, of course, not of this world, nor any longer "in" the world, in the sense of being-in-the-world: it is not worldly. Positioning itself outside the world, it gains, so to speak, a theological status. Here one can see the dependency of the representation of the world on onto-theology. The world is thus missed, passed over, in its representation, by onto-theology, and onto-theology reveals itself in the positioning a subject: "Even without a religious representation, such a subject, implicit or explicit, perpetuates the position of the creating, organizing, and addressing God (if not the addressee) of the world" (CW, 40). And in fact, the world outside of its representation "is above all a world without a God capable of being the subject of its representation" (CW, 43).

A second characteristic of the obscuring of the world is thus onto-theology, or what Nancy calls "the great transcendent accounts of rationalism" (CW, 41). Nancy would even identify "world-forming," that is, the immanent structure of the world—the fact that the world only refers to itself and never to another world (postulate of onto-theology)—as a "detheologization" (CW, 51). This will be, in effect, a leitmotif in Nancy's thought of the world: the world is an absolute immanence; we will return to this.

II

For Nancy, the world emerges as a proper philosophical problem against the background of a withdrawal of onto-theology, and its putting into play as an absolute existence is correlative to the disappearance of God. Becoming-world is thus the inverse of "theologization." In effect, what used to stand in the way of, or obstruct, a thought of the world (as absolute immanence and value) was the division of the totality of being according to the tripartite nature-man-God. God, for Nancy, amounts to this: another world placed next to this world, other than this world. "[F]or a God distinct from the world would be another world" (CW, 44–45).[6] God is what is outside the world. It is to that extent that the subject of representation was bound to theism. Now, the first proposition of an authentic thought of the world is that the world never refers to another world. Concerning the limits or the boundaries of the world, Nancy states, "[The world] never crosses over these edges to occupy a place overlooking itself" (CW, 43). And, if one "leaves this world," it is not to attain another world; it is simply no longer being-*in*-the-world, no longer being in a world, no longer having a world. To that extent, "this world" is the only world. Thus, to die is to leave the world, *as world*, and no longer to leave this world for another world. To no longer be is to no longer be in the world. This is why a world does not get crossed over (it does not have an outside), rather, it is traversed: from beginning to end, from one edge to another, but never in order to access an outside or a beyond, site of the divine. This is why the expression "the sense or meaning of the world [*le sens du monde*]," the title of one of Nancy's major works,[7] cannot signify the sense *of* the world as objective genitive, an encompassing of the world as totality on the basis of an external overview (following the formula of Wittgenstein, according

5

to which "the meaning of the world must be situated outside the world"), but, rather, a subjective genitive, produced from the internal references of the world ("Thus the meaning of the world does not occur as a reference to something external to the world" [CW, 43]). The world only refers to itself, and its meaning does not come from the outside, it "circulates," Nancy tells us, "between all those who stand in it, each time singular and singularly sharing a same possibility *that none of them, any place or any God outside of this world, accomplishes*" (ibid; our emphasis). It is in this sense that the world is not of the order of a substance, a support, or a basis: the world does not presuppose itself; it exists as an extension of itself, as gap from itself, without ground or against the background of nothing.[8] Thus, let us specify that when Nancy speaks of meaning, he does not intend by this term the same thing as "signification," in the sense of an accomplished given meaning, but rather the opening of the possibility of the production of significance.[9] Meaning is not given, it is to be invented, to be created, that is to say, as we will see, out of nothing, *ex nihilo* . . .

As we can see, Nancy's thought with respect to the world is a thought of an absolute immanence in opposition to the tradition of transcendence (position of an other world). And nevertheless, Nancy shows that the world, the question of the being-world of the world, operates within onto-theology; he shows that such onto-theology self-deconstructs and confirms, in spite of itself, the unity of the world and its radical immanence. He indeed writes that the classical thinking with respect to God "questioned the being-world of the world" (CW, 41). He states it very clearly: in classical onto-theology, in the end it was a matter of nothing else than the world. In fact, Nancy continues, "there is no need of a prolonged study to notice that, already in the most classical metaphysical representations of that God, nothing else was at stake, in the end, than the world itself, in itself, and for itself" (ibid.). What, in effect, did the classical transcendences of onto-theology provide an account of? The world. They provided its immanent structure, supplied "a reason internal to the general order of things" (CW, 44). God is effectively the God *of the world*, He is the subject of the world, of its fabrication, of its maintenance, and of its destination. Of the world, God was the creator, the organizer. In this sense, for Nancy, onto-theology would elaborate nothing other than "the immanent relation of the world to itself" (CW, 41). Is it a coincidence that in philosophy the "vertical" theological transcendence became replaced with Kant by a "horizontal" transcendence that is nothing other than the horizon and structure of the world itself? In Kant, we see to the position of the world as transcendental, that is, the very place for what appears and happens, or, as Nancy writes, the world appears in Kant's philosophy as "the place, dimension, and actuality of thought: the space-time of meaning and truth" (ibid.), and no longer simply as an object of vision (for the subject). Therefore, Nancy will locate a "becoming-world of the world," as he refers to it, in those classical figures of onto-theology that are the "continual creation" of Descartes (maintenance of the world), the *Dieu sive natura* of Spinoza (God as the world), etc. (Nancy also includes in this list Malebranche's "vision in God" and Leibniz's "monad of monads," internal logic of the world.) In each instance, it is a question of the world, of its truth and its meaning. It is to this extent that the question of the world will have formed the self-deconstruction that undermines onto-theology and that the god of metaphysics has merged with the world, indeed has become the world.

This god of metaphysics has become the world in the sense that the God of onto-theology has been "progressively stripped of the divine attributes of an independent existence, and only retained those of the existence of the world considered in its immanence" (CW, 44), which amounts to saying that the subject of the world (God) disappears in order for the world to appear *as subject*. In other words, the becoming-world of the world signifies that the world loses its status as object (of vision) in order to reach the status of subject (previously occupied by God as independent existence). Henceforth, there is nothing but the (immanent) world as subject of itself. That is to say, for Nancy, the world is always a relation to itself.[10] This relation to itself, as we noted above, does not proceed from a ground or a basis; it is an extension of itself, relating to itself from the proper extension of the world. Nancy writes:

> The God of onto-theology has produced itself (or deconstructed itself) as subject of the world, that is, as world-subject. In so doing, it suppressed itself as God-Supreme-Being and transformed itself, losing itself therein, in the existence for-itself of the world without an outside (neither outside of the world nor a world from the outside). (CW, 44)

God thus disappears, but He disappears *in the world*, which immediately means that we can no longer speak meaningfully in terms of being *within* the world [*dans-le-monde*] in the sense of what is contained within something else, but only in terms of being-*in*-the-world [*au-monde*]. The preposition "*au*," "in," explains Nancy, represents, in French, what now encapsulates the entire problem of the world. This shift from "within" to "in" indicates the radical immanence of the world: everything now takes place in the world, that is to say, right at the world, *à même* the world, as Nancy often writes. It is a matter for us of advancing in this proper thought of the world that deploys itself from the detheologization that we have only too briefly discussed. Nancy proceeds to expose the principal characteristics of the being-world of the world.

The first characteristic of the world is thus its radical immanence. The world no longer refers to a transcendence, to a beyond, to a god outside the world and distinct from the world; in short, the world no longer refers to another world: Nancy writes, "Whoever speaks of 'the world' renounces any appeal to 'another world' or a 'beyond-the-world' [*outre-monde*]" (CW, 37). This is why, in this original thought of the world, it is not a matter of a secularization of the theological: the world occurs outside of the theological scenario. It is no longer possible, in effect, to measure the meaning of the world by referring it to an external and transcendent model. The immanence of the world signifies, in the first place, that there is no model for the world, since the world is no longer reduced to or adjusted to a representation or to a principle: the world is *an-archic*. Without an exterior principle, it therefore can only refer to itself, and its meaning only arises from itself. It is absolutely free from all reference to an exterior: this is why the world's immanence is ab-solute, detached, without connection. Nancy thus speaks of "the" world, "absolutely"; this absolutization of the world being one of the senses of what we refer to as "world-forming." The world is an absolute, since it is no longer *relative* to another world. The sense of the world manifests this immanence, because the sense of the world is referred to a making-sense, which *is* the world as such: the world makes sense of itself by itself. The meaning is never a reference to an outside world, but only refers to itself, such a self-reference being the world. Thus, Nancy writes, "One could say that worldhood is the *symbolization* of the world, the way in which the world symbolizes in itself with itself, in which it articulates itself by making a circulation of meaning possible without reference to another world" (CW, 53).

The world manifests, therefore, an absolute immanence. The world is absolute, but nonetheless finite. It is finite, since, as we will see, it comes from nothing in order to return to nothing, and it is only itself a growth of/from nothing. The immanence of the world is therefore the conjunction of a finitude and of an absolute; it is an absolute finitude. This absolute finitude takes the form of an excess.

The world, no longer being a representation or a vision, manifests its mode of being as an excess with regard to this vision. The world exceeds its representation; it leaves it, and it appears outside this model, excessive, eccentric, and singular. Excess of a pure event, founded on nothing, outside representation, the world escapes from all horizons of calculability (in opposition to the logic of economic and technologic globalization). A world in excess has therefore the mode of being of an unpredictable event and for that reason cannot be the matter of a choice between possibilities. It would be rather, "a violent decision without appeal, because it decides between all and nothing—or, more precisely, it makes being something *in the place of nothing*" (CW, 59; our emphasis). Thus, it is a question of a decision for, "what is in no way given in advance, but which constitutes the eruption of the new, that is unpredictable because without face, and thus the 'beginning of a series of phenomena' by which Kant defines freedom in its relation to the world" (ibid.).

According to the very structure of any event, the world occurs in the incalculable, resistant to identity, according to what Derrida refers to as the possibility of the impossible. For Derrida, the impossible, which he writes as im-possible for reasons that will appear below, is possible and takes place as im-possible. In fact, the im-possible is, according to Derrida, which Nancy follows, the very structure of the event. The impossible, in this context, does not mean that which is not simply possible, and therefore without effect. The impossible, or the im-possible, means: that which happens outside the conditions of possibility offered in advance by a subject representation, outside the transcendental conditions of possibility, which, for Nancy, actually render impossible the subject of this experience of the world. We need to hold together the following two statements: *The transcendental makes experience impossible: the im-possible is the possibility of experience.* The world arrives as such an im-possible. Derrida often writes that an event or an invention is only possible as im-possible. This is why Nancy will specify, "Our question thus becomes clearly the question of the impossible experience or the experience of the impossible: an experience removed from the conditions of possibility of a finite knowledge, and which is nevertheless an experience" (CW, 65). This experience is the experience of the excess with respect to the conditions of anticipating possibilities. Experience takes place in the excess of the im-possible as the structure of the event.

The world is thus excessive, exceeding the conditions of possibility of representation and of the transcendental, but, nevertheless, establishing a proper stance. The world is without foundation (without representation), but it maintains a stance in this nothing: The world "[i]s essentially, not the representation of a universe (*cosmos*) nor that of a here below (a degraded world, if not condemned by Christianity), but the excess—beyond any representation of an *ethos* or a *habitus*—of a stance by which the world holds itself by itself, configures itself and exposes itself, refers to itself without referring to any given principle nor to any assigned end (CW, 47). This stance referred to in this passage by Nancy is an *ethos* and a *habitus*; it is also a *praxis*.

Nancy explains that the world, if it does not want to be a land of exile or a vale of tears, or simply the un-world [*immonde*] that it is becoming today, must be the place of a possible habitation. Above all, the world is a place. More precisely, it is the place of a possible taking-place, where there is "a genuine place, one in which things can genuinely *take place* (in this world)" (CW, 42). The world is the place of any taking-place, of any possible taking-place, the place where "there is room for everyone [*tout le monde*]" (ibid.). Nancy insists on this dimensionality of the world: the world "is nowhere"; it is, rather, "the opening of space-time" (CW, 73), a "spatio-temporal dis-positing dispersion," where everything can take-place, if it is the case that "what takes place takes place in a world and by way of that world" (CW, 42). The world is the place and the dimension of a possibility to inhabit, to coexist. The world "is only for those who inhabit it" (ibid.). It is a place for a proper taking-place and dwelling, because to take-place is not to simply occur but to properly arrive and happen. This properness indicates here the ethical dimension of the world, an originary ethics of being-of-the-world. Thinking together the stance of the world and the originary sense of *ethos* as dwelling, Nancy explains that the world is an *ethos*, a *habitus*, and a place of dwelling. It is also a *praxis*: the sense of the world is not given a priori, and our coexistence in the world is not given either, nor is it able to rely on any substantial basis. Not able to rely on any given, the world can thus only rely on itself. That is to say, the world suddenly appears from nothing . . . from itself. The sense of the world, not given, is to create, because "[t]he withdrawal of any given thus forms the heart of a thinking of creation" (CW, 69). The world, resting on nothing, is to invent in an original *praxis* of meaning; "meaning is always in *praxis*" (CW, 54), Nancy clarifies. It is never established as a given, it is never fulfilled or achieved; it is to be made and enacted. Being itself, as it is always "being without given," has the meaning of an act, of a making.

III

This making (sense) from *nothing given* is a creation *ex nihilo*, coming from nothing, and meaning, emerging from nothing, allows the world to appear as a nothing-of-given and as without-reason. Nancy poses, in recalling Heidegger's *Principle of Reason*, that, "neither reason nor ground sustains the world" (CW, 120, n.20). The world, not grounded on any principle, is a *fact*; it is only a fact (even if it is a singular fact, not being itself a fact *within* the world). It is not founded in reason, or in God. It is the fact of a "mystery," Nancy writes, the mystery of an accidental, errant or wandering existence (according to Wittgenstein, what is mystical is the *fact* that the world is). The world is neither necessary nor contingent, if contingency is defined in relation to necessity. Rather, it would be beyond or before necessity and of contingency, an absolute fact. It is possible to free the facticity of the world from the necessity-contingency conceptual couple by considering this fact of the world "without referring it to a cause (neither efficient nor final)" (CW, 45). The world is a fact without cause and without reason, it is "a fact without reason or end, and it is our fact" (ibid.). We are thus called, in this thought of the world as absolute immanence, to take on this facticity without reason of the world, as well as its non-sense, or rather that its sense only lies in such a fact: "To think it is to think this factuality, which implies not referring it to a meaning capable of appropriating it, but to placing in it, in its truth as a fact, all possible meaning" (ibid.). The world is a significance without a foundation in reason, or, as Nancy writes suggestively, a "resonance without reason" (CW, 47). The world is without reason, and is to itself its entire possible reason.

This facticity of the world is its abandonment, abandonment *by* and abandonment *to*. Nancy refers to this abandonment of the world as its *poverty*. The world is never a possession, but an abandonment: the world *is* poor. This poverty (which is not misery but the being-abandoned as such)[11] is due to the nothing that the world manifests: coming from nothing, resting on nothing, going to nothing,[12] the world is, writes Nancy in an striking passage, "the nothing itself, if one can speak in this way, or rather *nothing* growing [*croissant*] as *something*" (CW, 51). Noting the etymological links between growing [*croissant*], being born [*naître*], to grow [*croître*], *cresco*, and *creo*, Nancy introduces at this stage the motif of creation; to grow and to create: the movement of the world. "In creation, a growth grows from nothing and this nothing takes care of itself, cultivates its growth" (ibid.). Thus, in this sense, poverty grows.

The creation of which Nancy speaks, that is, the creation *of* the world (which is a subjective genitive), ought to be understood in a radical nontheological sense. It would even be, in its content and its logic, a nontheological notion, if it is the case that creating can only be *ex nihilo*, emergence from nothing, and not from God ("creation is a motif, or a concept, that we must grasp outside of its theological concept," Nancy insists [CW, 50]). Because the world rests on nothing, it exists *ex nihilo*, in a creation of itself. Creation lies entirely in the *ex nihilo* and not in the position of a theism, against which Nancy proclaims, not simply an a-theism, but an "absentheism" (ibid.). *God is absent in the creation of the world and disappears in the world.* Creation is no longer referred to theology, but to the *ex nihilo*,[13] which for its part is referred to a veritable *materialism*, if it is the case that the "*ex nihilo* is the genuine formulation of a radical materialism, *that is to say, precisely without roots*" (CW, 51; our emphasis).

Nancy engages this motif of creation to the exact extent that he takes leave with all reference to a given in his thought of the world: nothing is given, all is to be invented, to be created: "The world is created from nothing: this does not mean fabricated with nothing by a particularly ingenious producer. It means instead not fabricated, produced by no producer" (CW, 51). Thus, Nancy expresses that creation, in his thought, is "the exact opposite" (ibid.) of production, which supposes a given, a project, and a producer. Creation is without a transcendent creator (creation where the creator collapses and disappears, according to the logic of the auto-deconstruction of Christianity that we analyzed above),[14] a creation immanent to itself, a creation of itself, and from itself: "If the world is the growth of/from nothing—an expression of a formidable ambiguity—it is because it only depends on itself, while this 'self' is given from nowhere but from itself" (ibid.). The world is created from nothing, that is to say, as nothing, not in the sense of nothingness, but in the sense of nothing given and nothing of reason. The world emerges from nothing, is without precondition, without models, without given principle and end. Coming from nothing signifies: the presentation of nothing, not in the sense of a phenomenology of the unapparent or of negative theology, but in the sense where "that *nothing* gives itself and that *nothing* shows itself—and that this is." (CW, 123, n.24).

The creation of the world is thus that *praxis* of meaning and of dwelling, where there is a proper taking place, and it is such a creation of the world as an unpredictable appearance, as an eruption of the new, as absolute beginning, as dis-positing openness (the *ex* of *ex nihilo* as *différance*), as selfhood and coexistence (co- or with are "intricate" in the *ex*) that Nancy gives us to think about in these pages, world-forming as an alternative to globalization.[15] It is a matter of affirming and of willing the world, a world without foundation or founded on nothing, without reason, without end, without author and without subject, beyond representation: the only possibility of coming out of the un-world.

IV

The third part of *The Creation of the World* or *Globalization* opens the question of what one might call the undecidability of beginnings. One beginning with which Nancy is concerned in this text is the beginning of philosophy itself. On Nancy's account, philosophy begins from itself and evolves as a "technology of *logos*."[16] With this *self*-beginning, Nancy suggests that there is a "denaturation" of history. A natural history is interrupted, corrupted, or "denatured" by a philosophy that Nancy understands as a technology of *logos*, a technology that engenders metaphysics.[17] This self-beginning paradoxically arises out of the withdrawal of beginning: the withdrawal of beginning, Nancy explains, "belongs to self-beginning. The beginning remains ungrounded" (CW, 80). To that extent, the self-beginning is without principles or ends, and humans are henceforth fabricated through such technology, if technology is to be understood "as the planetary domination of the absence of beginning and end." The technology of *logos* thus reveals the denaturation of history, of the human being and of life itself. Life, Nancy insists, is no longer pure or bare, but rather produced according to technology. On Nancy's account, life becomes *technē*, and politics the management of *ecotechnology*.

Nancy's text, then, addresses the beginning of philosophy as a technology of *logos* that denatures history and human life. Even when it claims to be the other of all *technē*, even when it appeals to some ideality or naturalness, philosophy is irreducibly an original *technē*. And it is no accident, as Nancy reminds us, that philosophy from its inception has presented itself from the outset "as a dialogue with technologies or their meta-technological interpellation: beginning with Sophistry, and modeling itself on mathematics, the arts of the cobbler, the carpenter or in general" (CW, 89). As we will see, Nancy associates this self-beginning of philosophy with the phenomenon known as "globalization," the planetary domination of the process of denaturation brought about through technology. Nancy reveals the convergence of technology, metaphysics, and globalization, emphasizing that "metaphysics, as such, is essentially historical, accomplishes itself [*s'achève*] in the form of technology," and that "technology must be understood as the planetary domination of the absence of beginning and end, or of the withdrawal of any initial or final *given*—of any *phusis* or of any *muthos*" (CW, 81). The use of the term *de*naturation would imply, it seems, an originary state of *nature* that would have been *de*-natured; an original state to which one would have to return in order to restore one's proper nature. However, as much as such a reading might seem to be encouraged by the term *denaturation*, Nancy's intent is to reveal denaturation as such, that is, the withdrawal of principles and ends, the nothing of origins. Such a withdrawal has also another name: technology.[18]

The resource of the undecidability and groundlessness of beginnings is that *another* beginning, that is to say, other *beginnings*, would be possible. In fact, for Nancy, the beginnings of philosophy can only be written as plural, or even as "singular plural." This plurality ensues from the absence of ground. This is why he asks: "Is it possible to *make* history, to *begin again* a history—or History itself—on the basis of its non-foundation?" (ibid.). It is this possibility that the third section of *The Creation of the World* explores: not a particular beginning or a proper beginning as an alternative to philosophy's self-beginning, but the very *fact* and possibility of other beginnings. While the first beginning involves the denaturation of philosophy and the movement of globalization, Nancy gives thought to another event of creation, another distinctly different beginning that, in contrast with globalization, would be an authentic "world-forming." As we saw, the world that emerges in such an event of creation is not the world as an object, but rather a world that is indissociable from events of meaning. It is an issue, thus, of revealing the undecidability of beginnings so as to give thought to the fact of singular plural beginnings, a fact that as we will see constitutes the task and content of justice.

In the section of the text entitled "Creation as Denaturation: Metaphysical Technology," Nancy addresses the constitutive *aporia* of philosophy's beginnings. Nancy suggests that the seed of the beginning is contaminated and denatures the philosophical project. He writes:

> Philosophy begins as the self-productive technology of its name, of its discourse, and of its discipline. It engenders or it fabricates its own concept or its own Idea for itself at the same time that it invents or constructs these instrumental and ideal realities that are the "concept" and the "Idea." In this operation, the best known and most prominent feature is the differentiation of itself from what is called "sophistry": with respect to this technology of *logos*, philosophy defines itself and constitutes itself as that *technē* that is at the same time different from any other *technē* because it states first, or finally, its truth. In that very way, it invents itself also in its difference from any other knowledge, any other discipline, or any other science. With respect to this major difference, its *self-institution* is the key. (CW, 77; our emphasis)

As self-inaugural, philosophy is unable to give thought to its own beginning, since this self-beginning opens an *aporia*. Either it would posit a position from which it evolved (in which case it would not have begun from itself) or it proposes itself as an accident of the West, in which case, as Nancy asserts, it has no necessity (cf. CW, ibid.).

Nancy unfolds further *aporias* inherent in the relation between philosophy and history.[19] On the one hand, philosophy betrays history, he asserts, since history—if left unto itself—would be something without beginning and without end. Nancy writes, "There is thus a betrayal of the principle of history and of the world in the philosophical self-constitution and self-beginning" (CW, 79). As a *self*-beginning that conceives of its own ends, philosophy corrupts the natural history of the world and natural history must be excluded from its account.

On the other hand, Nancy suggests that philosophy *reveals* history, he writes:

> It is precisely by defining itself as an autonomous process and thus as history (philosophy *is* history and *makes* history as soon as Plato refers to its proper provenance in Anaxagoras, Parmenides, and Socrates) that philosophy unveils

14

the problematic order of an auto-constitution that must appropriate itself (that is to say, auto-constitute itself) through the mediation of its own temporal and genealogical difference along which the *auto-* alters itself primordially as much as it identifies itself. (CW, 79–80)

The *aporia* or chiasm, as Nancy refers to it, opens a space of uncertainty, inside and outside of history, a chronological time *of* history and a mythical time *outside* of history. In other words, the self-constituted duration carries its chronological time, and that which falls outside of this time is left to the nonphilosophical, or the mythical.

For Nancy, as we saw, a history that has begun itself from itself is deprived of ground, constituting the *aporia* of a beginning without reason and foundation: Yet, paradoxically, this withdrawal of ground is the very ground of the history that has begun from itself. "Is it possible or not to assume the non-foundation of the West as the reason for its own history? And since this history becomes the history of the world: is it possible or not to assume the non-foundation of the history of the world? This means: is it possible to *make* history, to *begin again* a history—or History itself—on the basis of its non-foundation?" (CW, 81). It is this lack of ground, this re-beginning and thus this undecidable, that Nancy reveals as he writes, "In this way, philosophy always institutes itself in a mixture of decision and indecision with respect to its own subject; and 'deconstruction' in sum is congenital for it since it constructs itself on the understanding that it must be anterior to its edifice and even to its own plan" (CW, 83).

The beginning on which Nancy dwells—which is neither the only one nor the last one—is that of philosophy as a technology of *logos*. It is this absence of beginning and "exhaustion of ends" that constitutes the "denaturation" of history and of meaning.

History is denatured to the extent that it no longer has a natural beginning or an end. "Truth—the truth of philosophy and of history—can do nothing else, henceforth, than open onto the abyss of its own beginning, or of its own absence of beginning, end, and ground" (CW, 82). There is consequently no end, no beginning, no future, and no possible anticipation.[20] Ends have been thought through to such an extent that they have been "exhausted" in the process. It is perhaps in the obsession of philosophy with the problematic of ends that the end loses any significance, as metaphysics accomplishes itself by wielding technology. Nancy explains as much in his interview recorded in the film *Der Ister* when he states that technology, lacking its own end, infinitely strives for an end, thereby erasing the meaning of end as such.[21]

V

On the basis of this beginning without principles or ends, and its attendant technology of *logos*, humans are themselves expressed or fabricated in technological modes. "There is a movement that is contemporary to human beings—technology as human, quite simply, *Homo faber*, producer and conceiver of *Homo sapiens*, technician of itself" (CW, 86). As history is denatured by a technology of *logos*, so is the human being, as can be seen particularly in the contemporary ethos of biopolitics and biopower.

Nancy states that the expression *biopolitics* designates the order of a politics devoted to the managing and control of life. Nancy's text draws, in this respect, on *The History of Sexuality Volume I: An Introduction*, by Michel Foucault.[22] Foucault writes of the focus on the body in the seventeenth century, a focus on the discipline and "extortion" of the body "as a machine," and on the biological processes (HS, 139). These two foci constitute a "*biopolitics of the population*," a "bipolar technology—anatomic and biological" whose "highest function was perhaps no longer to kill but to invest life through and through" (HS, 139). Further, for Foucault, this "biopower" was an important precursor to the development of industrial capitalism, which "would not have been possible without the controlled insertion of bodies into the machinery of production and the adjustment of the phenomena of population to economic processes" (HS, 141). These bioprocesses and conditions were facilitated by the development of socializing institutions, "(the family and the army, schools and the police, individual medicine, and the administration of collective bodies)" (HS, 141). These institutional techniques culminate in the conjunction of biological and political existence. Politics and power, as biopolitics and biopower, permeate, control, and transform every level and aspect of lived experience. It is this idea of the permeation and control of life by the technologies of biopolitics and power that Nancy discusses.

Nancy states that, except for the need for further investigations into the premodern forms of biopolitics, he has "nothing to add to this [Foucault's] historical thesis" (CW, 93). He asserts, in concert with Foucault, that "natural life" is "henceforth inseparable from a set of conditions that are referred to as 'technological' and which constitute what must rather be named *ecotechnology* where any kind of 'nature' develops for us (and by us). . . . It is in this context that a 'biopolitics' is possible, since it is defined by a technological management of life" (CW, 94). It is clear that for the most part Nancy shares Foucault's thinking in this context, including the view that "politics (still assigned to the State) progressively takes for its object the controlled management of natural life." However, Nancy challenges Foucault in the sense that he asks whether it is simply the case that "life" is the object of a controlling power. For Nancy, "life" does not offer a sufficiently philosophical problematic. "I believe it necessary however to ask if 'life' truly constitutes the object (real or imaginary, is not the issue now) of these powers, or if it is not rather is a destinal figure ('race' or 'the human worker') that comes to substitute for the classical figures of sovereignty. The reduction of these figures to 'life' is not sufficient to ground their political and affective power" (CW, 94).[23]

Nonetheless, Nancy emphasizes that, "what *forms a world* today is exactly the conjunction of an unlimited process of eco-technological enframing *and* of a vanishing of the possibilities of forms of life and/or of common ground" (CW, 95).

Michael Hardt and Antonio Negri also address Foucault's work in a similar vein, in their book *Empire*. Hardt and Negri echo Nancy's treatment of Foucault's philosophy and his critical thinking of the sovereign state of exception from which the world is controlled. Significantly, what is "created" from this sovereign position of the Empire is a "control that extends throughout the depths of the consciousnesses and bodies of the population—and at the same time across the entirety of social relations" (E, 24). Hence, it can be said that the sovereign creation of life as *technē* by biopolitics is a work of death. (Nancy speaks in this regard of a "total destruction [biological, ecological, ethological engineering]" [CW, 89].) Hardt and Negri state that with biopolitics "power is now exercised through machines that directly organize the brains (in communication systems, monitored activities, etc.) towards a state of autonomous alienation from the sense of life and the desire for creativity" (E, 23).[24] Following the section in *The Creation of the World* that addresses biopolitics, Nancy addresses the "sovereign" position from which the eco-technological enframing of human life operates.

VI

Nancy's problematic with respect to the question of sovereignty is developed in the section of the text entitled "*Ex Nihilo Summum* (Of Sovereignty)." In that chapter, Nancy endeavors to draw the contours of sovereignty, contours that are, as he puts it, outlined "around a hollow." Such a sovereignty, which he contrasts with domination and mastery, would be an "anti-sovereignty," a kind of "negative sovereignty," or a "sovereignty without sovereignty." That negative sovereignty is indeed marked by a hollow, a hollow that marks the absence of any theological foundation, the withdrawal of substantiality and subjectivity— one thinks here of his earlier work on *The Retreat of the Political*—in the very institution of sovereignty.[25] It also marks the nothing from which, *ex nihilo*, sovereignty is exercised, as it is no longer founded on anything but itself and its own creation, its own self-institution. "Instituting sovereignty," Nancy insists, "cannot be itself instituted. Better still, there is not, in a general way, an instituted sovereignty: *contradictio in adjecto*" (CW, 107). The sovereign, thus, "is the existent who depends on nothing." Indeed, Nancy contrasts an atheological sovereignty from traditional theologico-political sovereignty, stressing that the sovereign has no substantiality whatsoever, that it is based on nothing: its exercise "supposes that nothing either precedes it or supercedes it, that no authority or instituting force has been exercised before it. Sovereignty is the end of any political theology" (CW, 99). The sovereign is nothing except for what it creates. The invention of sovereignty is not "the secularized transcription of a political theology but the creation of an atheological assumption," Nancy writes evocatively.

Because of this detachment from any ground, sovereignty is to be thought of in terms of the exception to the law of which Carl Schmitt spoke. "The same condition that ensures that sovereignty receive its concept also deprives it of its power: that is, the absence of superior or foundational authority. For the sovereign authority must be essentially occupied with founding itself or with overcoming itself in order to legislate prior to or in excess of any law. In a rigorous sense, the sovereign foundation is infinite, or rather sovereignty is never founded. It would, rather, be defined by the absence of foundation or presupposition" (CW, 103). This is why the exercise of sovereignty takes place entirely under the condition of the "state of exception" where laws are suspended, betraying the fundamental illegitimacy of sovereignty as the condition of legitimacy having to legitimize itself. It is the exceptional position of sovereignty as a source of law, control, and power—itself outside the law, "prior to or in excess of any law"—that holds Nancy's attention. He seeks to interrogate the nonsubstantial source from which the sovereign operates, whether a medieval suzerain, an early modern sovereign, or a singular existence, as a site from which the creation of a world could ensue.[26]

Nancy undertakes a historical and philosophical analysis of the sovereign's situation of exception from which a "sovereign" operates, by drawing a distinction between a suzerain and a sovereign. The suzerain in the medieval world was *connected* to a lineage—from God to the eldest (even one who is deceased) to the suzerain. The sovereign, on Nancy's account, is detached, free to create the law and free to rule from above. It is absolute in the sense that it has no relation, no measure and no equivalence to anything or anyone.

This problematic of such an exceptional sovereignty is also central to Michael Hardt and Antonio Negri's *Empire*. For Hardt and Negri, the transcendent sovereign is an amorphous "Empire" that has no boundaries, limits, or particular territories. They assert that there is no center for the Empire. The Empire "suspends history and thereby fixes the states of affairs for eternity" (E, xiv).

Nancy's treatment (as well as that of Hardt and Negri) of sovereignty is also echoed in the work of Giorgio Agamben who has focused on the exception of the sovereign in *Homo Sacer: Sovereign Power and Bare Life*.[27] Agamben, in particular, reminds us of the crucial link between the concept of the state of exception and the political theory of the noted German jurist Carl Schmitt. For it was Schmitt who, in his text *Political Theology*, explicitly equated the sovereign with the state of exception, stating that the "Sovereign is he who decides on the exception."[28] For Agamben, this state of exception means that the sovereign power operates, as it were, outside of or above the law. It is the only and absolute law, as Agamben explains: "The state of exception is not a special kind of law (like the law of war); rather, insofar as it is a suspension of the juridical order itself, it defines law's threshold or limit concept" (SE, 4).

This contemporary discussion about "sovereignty" between Nancy, Agamben, and Negri and Hardt, does not spring from some arcane historical interest but out of a concernful engagement with Schmitt's corpus and the sovereign excesses that it seems to have justified and enabled. Agamben shows, for example, that, following Schmitt's works in the 1920s and early 1930s, "the Nazis spoke openly of a *gewollte Ausnahmezustand*, a 'willed state of exception,' for the purpose of establishing the National Socialist State'" (SE, 3). In *The Concept of the Political*, Schmitt defines politics in terms of a conflict between friend and enemy, or the "friend-enemy constellation," as he dubbed it.[29] In the same text, Schmitt speculates that the friend-enemy distinction can be applied to a domestic context, in which the government would identify its own people, or some group of its citizens, as the enemy (CP, 32). He propounds that "[e]very state provides, therefore, some kind of formula for the declaration of an internal enemy" (CP, 46). In *Legality and Legitimacy*, Schmitt thematizes, in a matter-of-fact manner, that the primary effect of the legal possession of power lies in the "proper use of the extraordinary powers in the state of exception."[30] The state of exception of which Schmitt spoke, and that the Nazis wielded, was provided and legitimized by Article 48 of the Weimar Constitution. Article 48 (Measures during the disturbance of security and order) provides that

> the President can utilize the necessary measures to restore public security and order, if necessary with the aid of armed force. For this purpose he may provisionally suspend, in whole or in part, the basic rights established in Articles 114, 115, 117, 118, 123, 124, 153. (LL, 103)

The "basic rights" established in Articles 114, 115, 117, 118, 123, 124, 153 included such matters as personal freedoms, domicilic sovereignty, freedom of expression, peaceful assembly, and others. Schmitt's theoretical reservations about the viability of parliamentary democracy and emphatic legitimation of the state of exception played all too well into the hands of Adolph Hitler. In fact, Hindenburg used Article 48 to suspend civil liberties after the February 27, 1933, Reichstag fire. Hitler then moved to tighten his grip on power.[31] Hitler outlawed his main political opposition and pushed both the Enabling Acts (March 23, 1933) and the Nuremberg Laws through parliament. Thus, through legal means and parliamentary procedures Hitler maneuvered himself into a "state of exception" provided by Article 48 and so thoroughly thematized by Schmitt, thus assuming absolute power.

The engagement by Nancy, Agamben, and Hardt and Negri of Carl Schmitt's concept of the political and his formulation of a state of exception, that is to say, a state of exception by which a government declares its own citizens to be the enemy and assumes emergency powers and takes action to eliminate the threat,[32] can also be read against the background of Jacques Derrida's seminal essay, "The Force of Law."[33] For it is in this text that Derrida addresses, among other topics, Schmitt and his relation to National Socialism. It is also in this text that Derrida raises the question of the ethics of deconstruction and its relation to responsibility and justice. Nancy's engagement of the question of the exceptional sovereign stands against this backdrop, while he provides his own interpretation. His intention is, in the end, to explore the undecidable resources of the position and the action of the sovereign. Nancy explores the extent to which the position of the sovereign or the subject of the sovereign could be the people, as in the case of a participatory democracy. He writes:

> The sovereign people possesses nothing less and nothing more than the absolute monarch: *namely, the very exercise of sovereignty.*
>
> This exercise is nothing other than the establishment of the State and of its law, or of the law that makes a State. It supposes that nothing either precedes it or supercedes it, that no authority or instituting force has been exercised before it. (CW, 99; our emphasis)

It is this resource of the sovereign (with the promise of the sovereignty of the people) that Nancy's project offers for further questioning. Nancy emphasizes that the sovereign is related only to itself and creates itself along with any of its institutions. He writes, "The sovereign does not find a sovereignty that is given: it must constitute it and thus constitute itself as sovereign" (CW, 100) For Nancy, then, the sovereign is thus in a state of *exception*, whether monarch, people, or singularity.

Through his analysis, Nancy seeks to approach the very possibility of sovereignty as the nonsubstantial place from which another beginning, another creation, another world (or a world anew) could ensue. In *The Creation of the World*, Nancy advances upon his proposition in *The Sense of the World* that the loss of the theological sovereign opens the possibility of a new sense of politics, and raises the question of how the sense of being-in-common can make itself "sovereign in a new way" (SW, 91). This new way could be formulated as follows: The sovereign is based on nothing: "no finality, no order of production or subjection, whether it concerns the agent or the patient or the cause or the effect. Dependent on nothing, it is entirely delivered over to itself, insofar as precisely, the "itself" neither precedes nor founds it but is the *nothing*, the very thing from which it is suspended" (CW, 103).

Nancy's thinking with respect to this possibility of a new sense of politics and justice is further developed in the concluding section of the book, entitled "*Cosmos Basileus*," a title that implies that a world or cosmos issues its own meaning from its own auto-constituted and therefore ungrounded sovereignty.

VII

Nancy insists that the world is subject to no authority, arising *ex nihilo*. He also marks that the unity of the world remains diverse, multiple. In this respect, he is able to claim that, "The sharing out [*partage*] of the world is the law of the world. The world does not have any other law, it is not submitted to any authority, it does not have any sovereign" (CW, 109). The law of the world is thus sharing, and this distribution, repartition, or attribution inherent in sharing opens the question and space of justice, the proper or appropriate attribution to each. "Territorial place, nourishment, a delimitation of rights and duties: to each and each time as appropriate." Justice is co-extensive with the sharing of the world and the appropriate part of each singularity (justice designates what must be rendered, restituted, returned, given in return to each singular existent). Now, this sharing, just like the world, is not given. Similarly, justice is not given, but to create; there lies the struggle for justice.

Nancy had already emphasized in *The Inoperative Community* that meaning is and can only be shared out. However, as inoperative as the community may be, the term *community* itself still suggested a coherence (the "common") that Nancy attempted to deconstruct. Hence the current text, *The Creation of the*

World, shifts from the vocabulary of "community" to a thinking of the world in terms of the singularity of creation as world-forming.

Yet there are crucial elements in the *Inoperative Community* that are present in *The Creation of the World* or *Globalization*. In *The Inoperative Community*, if using the term *community*, Nancy was challenging the immanence of commonality, or of a community of essence, as he termed it. To address this threat of immanence, associated with the threat of totalitarianism, Nancy has recourse to Heidegger's *Mitsein*, being-with, and *being-toward-death*, as a mode of finitude that is expressed in Dasein's radical singularity. For Nancy, what being-with and being-toward-death reveal is a sharing [*partage*] of singular existences. "The sharing itself is not a communion . . . nor even a communication as this is understood to exist between subjects. But these singular beings are themselves constituted by sharing, they are distributed and placed, or rather *spaced*, by the sharing that makes them *others*" (IC, 25).

For Nancy, in *The Inoperative Community*, community is composed of singular existences that "share" their singularity in their being toward death. "*Community*," he writes, "*does not sublate the finitude it exposes. Community itself, in sum, is nothing but this exposition*" (IC, 26). Such finite singularities are exposed to each other. Community is the co-sovereignty of singular beings. The exposition of singularity is what is "communicated" (IC, 29). But this communication is not, Nancy insists, a bond. Singularities are given without communion and without bond (ibid.).

For Nancy, this mutual exposure of the singularities is an undecidable tension from which the struggle for the creation of world must unfold. That struggle, in its singularity and the infinitely finite enactment of possible beginnings, is nothing less than, for Nancy, the condition and definition of justice.

> *To create the world* means: immediately, without delay, reopening each possible struggle for a world, that is, for what must form the contrary of a global injustice against the background of general equivalence. But this means to conduct this struggle precisely in the name of the fact that this *world* is coming out of nothing, that there is nothing before it and that it is without models, without principle and without given end, and that it is precisely *what* forms the justice and the meaning of a world. (CW, 54–55)

The suppression of such a creation of meaning, of "each possible struggle for a world," would constitute injustice. This openness to new beginnings, new creations, new worlds, is contrasted by Nancy with the "unworld" of the technology wielded by metaphysics and globalization. Nancy thematizes a world that is always already under formation and concludes that justice would be a world that is constituted by this inexhaustible creation of meaning.

In an attempt to oppose the empiric machine of eco-technology, then, Nancy offers the sovereignty of the world. Nancy suggests that the sovereignty of the world—*Cosmos Basileus*—reveals the excess of life with respect to controlled management. But what is ultimately at stake with this sovereign world in opposition to the control of bio-power is justice. For Nancy, the creation of the world (as a subjective genitive) is literally the work of justice. As world-forming, the world *is* justice-in-act. This justice is a justice that is appropriate, a justice that is due. What is appropriate to singularities in their being? The ultimate measure of appropriateness is exposure of singularities to one another. Nancy writes:

> But existence is nothing other than being exposed: expulsed from its simple self-identity and from its pure position, exposed to the event, to creation, thus to the outside, to exteriority, to multiplicity, to alterity, and to alteration. (In a sense, certainly, this is nothing other than being exposed to being itself, to its own "being" and also, consequently, being exposed as being: exposition as the essence of being.) (CW, 110)

Justice happens in the singular-plural expositions of existences and remains an inappropriable that is shared out by each but irreducible to a particular or a whole. Nancy asserts in this respect that "[j]ustice rendered to the singular plural is not simply a demultiplied or diffracted justice. It is not a unique justice interpreted according to perspectives or subjectivities—and nonetheless it remains the same justice, equal for all although irreducible and insubstitutable from one to the other" (CW, 61). This is an infinite justice, consequently, which must be rendered both to the propriety of each and the impropriety common to all: rendered to birth and to death, which hold between them the infinity of meaning. The world would be the justice of each creation for meaning. Justice would be a world constituted by this inexhaustible creation of meaning. This does not mean, however, that justice or meaning cannot be achieved, but means that each time it is enacted and each time it remains to be created or re-created.

In his essay "The Force of Law," Derrida suggested that deconstruction responds to a sense of responsibility without limits and is always "already engaged by this infinite demand of justice . . ." (FL, 19). Derrida is concerned with the *aporia* of law, an *aporia* whereby the establishment of a law, that is to say the exercise of the right to make law, abrogates the next act of lawmaking. And the subsequent act must overcome the previous (FL, 36). The act of lawmaking always involves an other and cuts with violence against the other. But for Derrida deconstruction allows us to recognize the instability and undecidability in the law and justice that renders it always "to come," a "to come" that would imply ongoing interpretation and re-creation.

For Nancy, this freedom of a sovereign creation of meaning is at its core radically undecidable. He writes of "the insatiable and infinitely finite exercise that is the being in act of meaning brought forth in the world [*mis au monde*]" (CW, 55). It is the measure of the resources of Nancy's philosophical work that the text explores the dimensions of this undecidability of creations, of such "infinitely finite" beginnings. Such is the resource of the undecidable: any beginning could not be the only beginning or the last. Nancy opens a space of interrogation between at least two beginnings: on the one hand, the self-beginning of philosophy that denatures history and humanity (globalization), and, on the other hand, the possibility of other beginnings that enact the world of justice through the plurality of beginnings. Nancy's articulation of the undecidability of beginnings opens a space for the reflection on a beginning that would lead to the creation of a world synonymous with justice.

As a book, *The Creation of the World* or *Globalization* enacts the singular and plural beginnings that Nancy associates with justice. The book is indeed organized around separate sections in which Nancy himself begins again, *à nouveau*, with each discussion. The plural beginnings in the text, "*Urbi et Orbi*," "Of Creation," "Creation as Denaturation: Metaphysical Technology," "Note on the Term *Biopolitics*," "*Ex Nihilo Summum* (Of Sovereignty)," and "*Cosmos Basileus*," each enact a performative portrayal of singular plural beginnings. Section I ("*Urbi et Orbi*"), for example, evokes the beginnings of the Christian world, on the one hand, and a Marxist worldview, on the other, as Nancy speculates on these dimensions of the becoming-world of the world. The creation portended by Marx was a world that is not beyond the world but a world "in fact," insofar as it is created "each time," a world that is outside of representation and without God, as discussed earlier.

> And if our world is neither necessary nor contingent, or if it is both at once, what does that mean? More generally, how does one disentangle oneself from this conceptual couple? Perhaps by considering a fact without referring it to a cause (neither efficient nor final). The world is such a fact: it may well be that it is the only fact of this kind (if it is the case that the other facts take place within the world). It is a fact without reason or end, and it is our fact. (CW, 45)

As noted earlier, what is central to the singularity of the plural beginnings is that the beginnings or creations come from a nothing that arises, as he emphasizes, "without-reason" and grows "of/from nothing": in this first section, what is at stake is not seizing the means of production with Marx but the creation of the world. This struggle for creation is, Nancy writes, "precisely *what* forms the justice and the meaning of a world" (CW, 55).

Following this beginning of the text, "*Urbi et Orbi*," Nancy begins again in the second section, "Of Creation," with an engagement with Kant, through Lyotard, of the relation of judgment to beginnings and ends. More precisely, Nancy is concerned with the judgment about ends, about what is never actually given in advance, but constitutes the eruption of the new and the unpredictable. For Nancy, Kant's *Critique of Judgment* presents us with yet another creation paradigm and is intrinsic to the philosophical project: its birth certificate: "The judgment about ends or about the end, about a destination or about a meaning of the world is the engagement of a philosophy (*or* about what one calls a "life") ever since an end is not given: this is the birth certificate of philosophy and of our so-called 'Western' or 'modern' history" (CW, 59).

Reflective judgment, for its part, is considered by Nancy as a mode in which a world is not constructed but *created*. Reflective judgment is the judgment of a particular for which no concept exists. But more important than the claim that the universal is not given in the reflective judgment, is the recognition that what is actually missing is not the concept of a reality, but the very existence of that reality as given. The issue is thus not to construct, but to create. Nancy writes:

> The "Idea," to use this Kantian-Lyotardian lexicon, is no longer a concept used in an analogical or symbolic mode outside of the limits of possible experience or of given intuition. It is no longer a concept without intuition, handled by virtue of something that substitutes for a sensible given: it becomes itself the creation of its own scheme, that is to say, of a novel reality, which is the form/matter of a world of ends. (CW, 62)

Nancy thus appropriates this discourse of reflective judgment insofar it points to the creation of the world, under no concept, whether already given or to construct. Hence, he seeks to articulate a third form of judgment that would be a creation out of the nothing (*ex nihilo*), a "judgment of a reason to which is given in advance neither end(s) nor means, nor anything that constitutes whatever kind of 'causality known to us'" (CW, 66). Ultimately, Nancy evokes a judgment about ends without any given criteria, but which is by itself the ethos and praxis of its own finality. Such an experience, as Nancy calls it, would be an experience removed from conditions of possibility, and hence the impossibility of experience or experience of the impossible of which Derrida speaks.

As Nancy asserts, in the book's other "beginnings" such "Creation as Denaturation: Metaphysical Technology," "*Ex Nihilo Summum* (Of Sovereignty)," or

"*Cosmos Basileus*," we are in a time in which ends have been exhausted, and it is for us to decide, to begin again. We encounter the position of the undecidability of beginnings, as the singular plural existences of the world, stand in relation to creation as "sovereign." We belong to the world, but in an ecstatic and singular plural manner, described suggestively by Giorgio Agamben as a state of "ecstasy belonging, " the "topological structure of the state of exception" (SE, 35). Such a "topological structure" entails, for Agamben "*being-outside and yet belonging*" (SE, 35).[34] Perhaps this topological structure articulates the sharing-out of singular plural existences that is central to Nancy's thinking of the world as justice. Such is the possibility that Jean-Luc Nancy's *The Creation of the World or Globalization*, invites us to think.

Author's Prefatory Note
to the English Language Edition

Note on the Untranslatable *Mondialisation*

It is not without paradox that in many languages the French term *mondialisation* is quite difficult to translate, and that perhaps this difficulty makes it almost "untranslatable" in the sense that the term has acquired in the recent *Vocabulaire européen des philosophies*. This difficulty lies in the fact that the English term *globalization* has already established itself in the areas of the world that use English for contemporary information exchange (which is not necessarily symbolic exchange). There are therefore at least two terms (this being said without being able to take into account a considerable number of languages, which would introduce a supplementary perspective—which of course would be impossible)—two terms to designate the phenomenon that understands itself or seeks to be understood as a unification or as a common assumption of the totality of the parts of the world in a general network (if not a system) of communication, commercial exchange, juridical or political reference points (if not values), and finally of practices, forms, and procedures of all kinds linked to many aspects of ordinary existence.

The French language has used the word *mondialisation* since the middle of the twentieth century—which seems to me slightly before the term *globalization* appeared in English. The reasons for this neologism should be studied for their own sake. Whatever those reasons may be, the connotation of the term *mondialisation* gives it a more concrete tonality than that of *globalisation*, which designates, in French, a more abstract process leading to a more compact result: the "global" evokes the notion of a totality as a whole, in an indistinct integrality.

Thus, there has been in the English *globalization* the idea of an integrated total-ity, appearing for example with the "global village" of McLuhan, while *mondial-isation* would rather evoke an expanding *process* throughout the expanse of the *world* of human beings, cultures, and nations.

The usage of either term, or the search for an English translation that would keep the semantics of "world"[1] are not without a real theoretical inter-est: the word *mondialisation*, by keeping the horizon of a "world" as a space of possible meaning for the whole of human relations (or as a space of possible significance) gives a different indication than that of an enclosure in the undif-ferentiated sphere of a unitotality. In reality, each of the terms carries with it an interpretation of the process, or a wager on its meaning and future. This also means that it is understandable that *mondialisation* preserves something untrans-latable while *globalization* has already translated everything in a global idiom.

Jean-Luc Nancy, December 2004

Author's Prefatory Note
to the French Language Edition

"The creation of the world *or* globalization": the conjunction must be understood simultaneously and alternatively in its disjunctive, substitutive, or conjunctive senses.

According to the first sense: between the creation of the world or globalization, one must choose, since one implies the exclusion of the other.

According to the second sense: the creation of the world, in other words globalization, the former must be understood as the latter.

According to the third sense: the creation of the world or globalization, one or the other indifferently, leads us to a similar result (which remains to be determined).

The combination of these three senses amounts to raising the same question: can what is called "globalization" give rise to a world, or to its contrary?

Since it is not an issue of prophesizing nor of controlling the future, the question is, rather, how to give ourselves (open ourselves) in order to look ahead of ourselves, where nothing is visible, with eyes guided by those two terms whose meaning evades us—"creation" (up to this point limited to theological mystery), "world-forming" [*mondialisation*] (up to this point limited to economic and technological matters, generally called "globalization").

creation
world forming } *beyond God*
+ economy
technology } (1)

29

I

Urbi et Orbi

Urbi et orbi: this formulation drawn from papal benediction has come to mean "everywhere and anywhere" in ordinary language. Rather than a mere shift in meaning, this is a genuine disintegration. This disintegration is not simply due to the dissolution of the religious Christian bond that (more or less) held the Western world together until around the middle of a twentieth century to which the nineteenth century effectively relinquished its certainties (history, science, conquering humanity—whether this took place with or against vestiges of Christianity). It is due to the fact that it is no longer possible to identify either a city that would be "The City"—as Rome was for so long—or an orb that would provide the contour of a world extended around this city. Even worse, it is no longer possible to identify either the city or the orb of the world in general. The city spreads and extends all the way to the point where, while it tends to cover the entire orb of the planet, it loses its properties as a city, and, of course with them, those properties that would allow it to be distinguished from a "country." That which extends in this way is no longer properly "urban"—either from the perspective of urbanism or from that of urbanity—but megapolitical, metropolitan, or co-urbational, or else caught in the loose net of what is called the "urban network." In such a network, the city crowds, the hyperbolic accumulation of construction projects (with their concomitant demolition) and of exchanges (of movements, products, and information) spread, and the inequality and apartheid concerning the access to the urban milieu (assuming that it is a dwelling, comfort, and culture), or these exclusions from the city that for a long time has produced its own rejections and outcasts, accumulate proportionally. The result can only be understood in terms of what is called an *agglomeration*, with its senses of conglomeration, of piling up, with the sense of accumulation that, on the one hand, simply concentrates (in a few neighborhoods, in a few houses, sometimes in a few protected mini-cities) the well-being that used to be urban or civil, while on the other hand, proliferates what bears the quite simple and unmerciful name of misery.

This network cast upon the planet—and already around it, in the orbital band of satellites along with their debris—deforms the *orbis* as much as the *urbs*. The agglomeration invades and erodes what used to be thought of as *globe* and

33

The GLOMUS
unequal; technoscience
econ/biol/cult

which is nothing more now than its double, *glomus*. In such a *glomus*, we see the conjunction of an indefinite growth of techno-science, of a correlative exponential growth of populations, of a worsening of inequalities of all sorts within these populations—economic, biological, and cultural—and of a dissipation of the certainties, images, and identities of what the world was with its parts and humanity with its characteristics.

Hegels skepticism leading to renewed

The civilization that has represented the universal and reason—also known as the West—cannot even encounter and recognize any longer the relativity of its norms and the doubt on its own certainty: this was already its situation two centuries ago. (Hegel wrote in 1802: "[T]he increasing range of acquaintance with alien peoples under the pressure of natural necessity; as, for example, becoming acquainted with a new continent, had this skeptical effect upon the dogmatic common sense of the Europeans down to that time, and upon their indubitable certainty about a mass of concepts concerning right and truth.")[1]

future no longer possible

This skepticism, in which Hegel saw the fecundity of the destabilization of dogmatisms today, no longer harbors the resource of a future whose dialectic would advance reason farther, ahead or forward, toward a truth and a meaning of the world. On the contrary, it is in the same stroke that the confidence in historical progress weakened, the convergence of knowledge, ethics, and social well-being dissipated, and the domination of an empire made up of techno-logical power and pure economic reason asserted itself. *empire of technolo power + econ. reason*

yet no other challenges to this West

The West has come to encompass the world, and in this movement it disappears as what was supposed to orient the course of this world. For all that, up until now, one cannot say that any other configuration of the world or any other philosophy of the universal and of reason have challenged that course. Even when, and perhaps especially when one demands a recourse to the "spiritual," unless it is to the "revolution" (is it so different?), the demand betrays itself as an empty wish, having lost all pretense of effective capacity, or else as a shameful escape—and even when it does not appear as a supplementary means of exploiting the conditions created by the economic and technological exploitation. (To take what is "positive" of the West and to infuse it with something new—"values"—on the basis of an African, Buddhist, Islamic, Taoist, perhaps supra-Christian or supra-communist soul, such has been for a long time the sterile theme of many a dissertation . . .).

The world has lost its capacity to "form a world" [*faire monde*]: it seems only to have gained that capacity of proliferating, to the extent of its means, the "unworld" [*immonde*],[2] which, until now, and whatever one may think of retrospective illusions, has never in history impacted the totality of the orb to such an extent. In the end, everything takes place as if the world affected and permeated itself with a death drive that soon would have nothing else to destroy than the world itself.

proliferation of an unworld.

World cannot form itself.

34

It is not a question of "weighing in" for or leaning toward either the destruction or the salvation. For we do not even know what either can signify: neither what another civilization or another savagery arising out of the ruins of the West might be, nor what could be "safe/saved" when there is no space outside of the epidemic (in this respect, AIDS is an exemplary case, as are certain epizootic diseases on another level: the scale of the world, of its technologies and of its *habitus*, brings the terror of the plagues of the past to incommensurable heights).

The fact that the world is destroying itself is not a hypothesis: it is in a sense the fact from which any thinking of the world follows, to the point, however, that we do not exactly know what "to destroy" means, nor which world is destroying itself. Perhaps only one thing remains, that is to say, one thought with some certainty: what is taking place is really happening, which means that it happens and happens to us in this way more than a history, even more than an event. It is as if being itself—in whatever sense one understands it, as existence or as substance—surprised us from an unnamable beyond. It is, in fact, the ambivalence of the unnamable that makes us anxious: a beyond for which no alterity can give us the slightest analogy.

It is thus not only a question of being ready for the event—although this is also a necessary condition of thought, today as always. It is a question of owning up to the present, including its very withholding of the event, including its strange absence of presence: we must ask anew what the world wants of us, and what we want of it, everywhere, in all senses, *urbi et orbi*, all over the world and for the whole world, without (the) capital[3] of the world but with the richness of the world.

Let us begin with a lengthy citation to which we must give our sustained attention:

> In history up to the present it is certainly an empirical fact that separate individuals have, with the broadening of their activity into world-historical activity, become more and more enslaved under a power alien to them (a pressure which they have conceived of as a dirty trick on the part of the so-called world spirit [*Weltgeist*], etc.), a power which has become more and more enormous and, in the last instance, turns out to be the world market. But it is just as empirically established that, by the overthrow of the existing state of society by the communist revolution (of which more below) and the abolition of private property which is identical with it, this power, which so baffles the German theoreticians, will be dissolved; and that then the liberation of each single individual will be accomplished in the measure in which history becomes transformed into world history. From the above it is clear that the

are we destroying the world?

real intellectual wealth of the individual depends entirely on the wealth of his real connections. Only then will the separate individuals be liberated from the various national and local barriers, be brought into practical connection with the material and intellectual production of the whole world and be put in a position to acquire the capacity to enjoy this all-sided production of the whole earth (the creation of man).[4]

Marx on world creation

This text from *The German Ideology* dates from the time that is considered, not without reason, as that of the "early" Marx: he nevertheless formulates what was his conviction to the end according to which "communism" is nothing other than the actual movement of world history insofar as it becomes global and thus renders possible, and perhaps necessary, the passage to consciousness and enjoyment of human creation in its entirety by all human beings. Human beings would henceforth be freed from what limited the relation in which they mutually produce themselves as spirit and as body. In other words, it was his conviction that humanity is defined by the fact that it produces itself as a whole—not in general, but according to the concrete existence of each, and not in the end only humans, but with them the rest of nature. This, for Marx, is the world: that of the market metamorphosing itself or revolutionizing itself in reciprocal and mutual creation. What Marx will define later as "individual property," that is to say, neither private nor collective, will have to be precisely the property or the proper of each as both created and creator within this sharing of "real relations."

world produces itself as a whole — world relations

Thus, for Marx, globalization and the domination of capital converge in a revolution that inverts the direction [*sens*] of domination—but which can do so precisely because the global development of the market—the instrument and the field of play of capital—creates in and of itself the possibility of revealing the real connection between existences as their real sense. The commodity form, which is the fetishized form of value, must dissolve itself, sublimate or destroy itself—in any case revolutionize itself, whatever its exact concept—in its true form, which is not only the creation of value but value as creation. Transcribed in terms closer to our current linguistic usage (if we retain the distinction of senses between "globalization" [*globalisation*][5] and "world-forming" [*mondialisation*]—a distinction that sometimes in France in particular encompasses two usages of the same word *mondialisation*—these semantic complexities are the indicators of what is at stake): globalization makes world-forming possible, by way of a reversal of global domination consisting in the extortion of work, that is, of its value, therefore of value, absolutely. But if globalization has thus a necessity—the necessity that Marx designated as the "historical performance" of capital and that consists in nothing other than the creation by the

capital revolutionizes the world)

Globalization — creation of world

market of the global dimension as such—it is because, through the interdependence of the exchange of value in its merchandise-form (which is the form of general equivalency, money), the interconnection of everyone in the production of humanity as such comes into view.

If I may focus even more on this point: commerce engenders communication, which requires community, communism. Or: human beings create the world, which produces the human, which creates itself as absolute value and enjoyment [*jouissance*] of that value.

Consequently, the "communist revolution" is nothing other than the accession of this global connection to consciousness and through it the liberation of value as the real value of our common production. It is the becoming-conscious and the mastery in act of the self-production of human beings in the twofold sense of the production of human quality ("total humanity," free producer of freedom itself) and of the production of each by the others, all by each and each by all ("total humanity," as circulation of value freed from equivalence, circulation of the value that responds to the human being itself, each time singular, and perhaps also to others, or to all other existents as singular).

Certainly, each of the determinative concepts of this interpretation of the history of the world appears to us today as what we know to be its fragility: process, consciousness, the possibility of uncovering a value and an end in itself. We could note that these concepts are not those upon which Marx constructs his argument explicitly: they rather subtend his argument. But what diminishes their role also reveals their uncontrolled and hidden presence. Whatever the case, something remains nonetheless, in spite of everything, something resists and insists: there remains, on the one hand, precisely what happens to us and sweeps over us by the name of "globalization," namely, the exponential growth of the globality (dare we say *glomicity*) of the market—of the circulation of everything in the form of commodity—and with it of the increasingly concentrated interdependence that ceaselessly weakens independencies and sovereignties, thus weakening an entire order of representations of belonging (reopening the question of the "proper" and of "identity"); and there remains, on the other hand, the fact that the experience undergone since Marx has increasingly been the experience that the place of meaning, of value, and of truth is the world. Whoever speaks of "the world" renounces any appeal to "another world" or a "beyond-the-world" [*outre-monde*]. "World-forming" also means, as it does in this text from Marx, that it is in "this" world, or as "this" world—and thus as the world, absolutely—that what Marx calls production and/or the creation of humanity, is being played out.[6]

Our difference with him nonetheless reappears on this very point: with him, "human" implicitly remains a teleological or eschatological term, if we understand by that a logic where the *telos* and/or the *eschaton* take the position and the role of an accomplishment without remainder. For Marx, the human being, as source and accomplishment of value in itself, comes at the end of history when it produces itself: the source must therefore end entirely spread out and accomplished. For us, on the contrary, "the human being" is reduced to a given principle, relatively abstract ("person," "dignity") and as such distinct from an actual creation. In truth, it is the figure of "the human being" and with it the configuration of "humanism" that are erased or blurred while we have, at the same time, the most compelling reasons not to replace them with (the figures of) "the overman" or "God."

It is, however, not certain that with Marx the teleo-eschatological logic is so strictly geared toward the accomplishment of a final value. In a sense, it is even the determination of such a finality that remains lacking in Marx (if the absence of a finality is a lack at all . . .)—and this is perhaps what produced all sorts of myth-producing interpretations. In Marx's entire text, nothing determines, in the end, any accomplishment except as, essentially open and without end, a freedom ("free labor") and a "private property" (that which is proper to each in the exchange of all). But what, since Marx, has nonetheless remained unresolved [*en souffrance*]—and we know what "suffering" means here—is precisely the grasping of a concrete world that would be, properly speaking, the world of the proper freedom and singularity of each and of all without claim to a world beyond-the-world or to a surplus-property (in another capital). Quite to the contrary, the world which, for Marx, could be the space of the play of freedom and of its common/singular appropriation—the infinity in act of proper ends—only appears to us as a bad infinite, if not as the imminence of a finishing that would be the implosion of the world and of all of us in it.

At this point, it is necessary to clarify the nature of absolute *value* in itself: the one that Marx designates as "value" pure and simple, not a use-value of which exchange-value is the phenomenal mask and social extortion or exploitation.[7]

Much attention is usually given to "commodity fetish," the concept and/or representation of which are certainly important; but this also risks fetishizing this "fetishism" and risks making it the open secret of commodity. Now we must distinguish two perspectives: the first is that of the phenomenality of value (of "meaning" or of "the human"), a phenomenality that the "fetish" can make us forget (by reducing it to a religious mystification)[8] that it probably pertains to a general law according to which value or meaning can only be (re)presented,[9] even if not strictly speaking "fetishized." The other perspective—the only one I will consider here—is the one that must consider value as such, the "thing in itself" behind the phenomenon.[10]

Absolute value is, in fact, humanity incorporated in the product through work as human work. It is thus humanity producing itself by producing objects (or, I will return to this, creating itself by producing).[11] But what is humanity? What is the world as the product *of human beings*, and what is the human being insofar as it is *in the world* and as it *works* this world? What is the "spiritual richness" of which Marx speaks, which is nothing other than the value or meaning of human labor as human, that is to say, also, "free," but free to the extent that it is to itself its own end and that therefore it is neither value measured according to its use nor value giving itself as general equivalency (*it too is its own end*, but abstract and formal, a finality *for itself* . . .)? What is a value that is neither finalized nor simply equivalent to itself? What is a "human value" toward which the work refers, or whose trace it bears, without however signifying it and without covering it with a mystical veil? (This question, we note, amounts to asking: What is human value considered at a level beyond the reach of "humanism"?).[12]

Perhaps by considering its inverted figures one can approach this value. On September 11, 2001, we witnessed the collision, in the symptom and symbol of the clash, between the United States (summarized in the name, heavy with meaning, of "World Trade Center") and Islamic fanaticism, two figures of absolute value that are also—not surprisingly—two figures of monotheism. On the one hand, the God whose name is inscribed on the dollar, and on the other, the God in whose name one declares a "holy war." Of course, both Gods are instrumentalized. But I neglect here the examination of the instrumental logic that is latent, at least, in every religion. It remains that these two figures proceed from the same unique God (or from the same One taken as God) and expose the enigmatic sameness of the One that is, no doubt, always self-destructive: but self-destruction is accompanied by self-exaltation and an over-essentialization.

Let us keep in mind in any case that these two figures present absolute value as all-powerfulness and as all-presence of this all-powerfulness. Value is therefore first itself instrumentalized therein: it serves the reproduction of its own power, indefinitely, through spiritual or monetary capitalization. Value has value through this endless autistic process, and this infinite has no other *act* than the reproduction of its *potentiality* (thus in both senses of the word, power and potentiality). The "bad infinite," following Hegel, is indeed the one that cannot be *actual*.[13] On the contrary, the enjoyment of which Marx speaks, implies, as for any enjoyment, its actuality, that is to say, also the finite inscription of its infinity. It is not power that wills power, nor presence that insists in itself, but the suspension of will, the withdrawal, if not the fault, that marks enjoyment as enjoyment of a truth or of a sense, of a "spiritual wealth" or a "beatitude" in Spinoza's sense (that is to say, as an exercise, as the act of a relation to the totality of meaning or truth).

Power founds itself on itself as if on a reason that is always sufficient with respect to its exercise, even if destructive and self-destructive. Enjoyment does not give an account of itself. It is in this actuality without reason or end (no doubt the "free labor" of which Marx spoke) that value can be incommensurable, unable to be evaluated, to the point of no longer being a "value" and becoming what the German calls *Würde*, beyond the *Wert*, and which we translate as "dignity."

The question posed by the world in formation is this one: how to do justice to the infinite in act, of which infinite potentiality is the exact reverse?

When the bad infinite appears to be clearly without end, completely unbound (having rid itself of its teleological humanism), then this question imposes itself, stark and blinding. To reverse an infinite into another, and potentiality into act, is what Marx calls "revolution." It is necessary, in the end, that the world has absolute value for itself—or else that it has no value whatsoever, as the two forms of all-powerfulness, which have nothing but contempt for the world, indicate. It is in the end necessary that the infinite reason that gives an account of itself allows the actual without-reason (or actual existence) to appear—or that it liquidates itself in its disastrously interminable process.

One may assume that the problem of the apprehending of the world (of its absolute value) is posed in the following way: the world takes place, it happens, and everything seems as if we did not know how to apprehend it. It is our production and our alienation. It is not an accident if, since Marx, the "world" and the "worldly" [*le mondial*] have remained uncertain determinations, overly suspended between the finite and the infinite, between a new and former world, between this world and an other: in short, one may assume that the "world" has fallen short of what it should be, of what it can be, perhaps of what it already is, in some way that we have not yet determined. And it is probably due as well to the fact that "the world" has been secondary to the concept of a world "view" (it was no accident that a *Weltanschauung* played by accident a major political and ideological role in Nazism). It is as if there was an intimate connection between capitalistic development and the capitalization of views or pictures of the world (nature + history + progress + consciousness, etc.—all "views" gathered in a picture whose composition henceforth is blurred and runs on the canvas).

A world "viewed," a represented world, is a world dependent on the gaze of a subject of the world [*sujet du monde*]. A subject of the world (that is to say as well a subject of history) cannot itself be within the world [*être dans le monde*]. Even without a religious representation, such a subject, implicit or explicit, perpetuates the position of the creating, organizing, and addressing God (if not the addressee) of the world.

- value that can no longer be evaluated; beyond value.
- need to reverse bad infinity, 40 into another, make pot. an act.
  REVOLT
- world reduced to worldview → capitalist development and → religious capitalization of world. view of world

And yet, remarkably, there is no need of a prolonged study to notice that, already in the most classical metaphysical representations of that God, nothing else was at stake, in the end, than the world itself, in itself and for itself. In more than one respect, it is legitimate to say that the great transcendent accounts of rationalism elaborated nothing else than the immanent relation of the world to itself: they questioned the being-world of the world. I only ask, in passing, that one reflect on the sense of "continual creation" in Descartes, on that of Spinoza's *Deus sive natura*, on the "vision in God" in Malebranche or on the "monad of monads" with Leibniz. It would not be inaccurate to say that the question of the world—that is to say, the question of the necessity and meaning of the world—will have formed the self-deconstruction that undermines from within onto-the-ology.[14] It is such a movement that made possible, after Kant who was the first to explicitly confront the world as such (and, in sum, did nothing else), not only the entry of the world into thought (as an object of vision), but its emergence as the place, the dimension and actuality, of thought: the space-time of meaning and truth. In this respect, Marx's insistence on the world—an insistence that empha-sizes both the "worldwide" (coexistence) and the "worldly" (immanence)—is itself a decisive advance of the self-deconstructive gesture. (In this respect, and however paradoxical it may seem, it is indeed in Husserl and Heidegger that it continued, and as well as, albeit differently, in Bergson and Wittgenstein.)

In any case, the decisive feature of the becoming-world of the world, as it were—or else, of the becoming-world of the whole that was formerly articu-lated and divided as the nature-world-God triad—is the feature through which the world resolutely and absolutely distances itself from any status as object in order to tend toward being itself the "subject" of its own "world-hood"—or "world-forming." But being a subject in general means having to become oneself . . .

In order to grasp once more what is at stake in the question of the world as it presents itself to us in this way, let us consider the question of the concept in its simplest form: What is a world? Or what does "world" mean?

Briefly, I would say first: a world is a totality of meaning. If I speak of "Debussy's world," of "the hospital world," or of the "fourth world," one grasps immediately that one is speaking of a totality, to which a certain meaningful content or a certain value system properly belongs in the order of knowledge or thought as well as in that of affectivity and participation. Belonging to such a totality consists in sharing this content and this tonality in the sense of "being familiar with it," as one says; that is to say, of apprehending its codes and texts, precisely when their reference points, signs, codes, and texts are neither explicit nor exposed as such. A world: one finds oneself in it [*s'y trouve*] and one is familiar with it [*s'y retrouve*]; one can be in it with "everyone" ["*tout le monde*"], as we say in French. A world is precisely that in which there is room for everyone: but a genuine place, one in which things can genuinely *take place* (in this world). Otherwise, this is not a "world": it is a "globe" or a "glome," it is a "land of exile" and a "vale of tears."

From this brief characterization a few implications follow.

First, a world is not a unity of the objective or external order: a world is never in front of me, or else it is not my world. But if it is absolutely other, I would not even know, or barely, that it is a world. (For instance, for me, a few fragments of Hittite art do not even suggest the *world* of that art.) As soon as a world appears to me as a world, I already share something of it: I share a part of its inner resonances. Perhaps this term *resonance* is capable of suggesting the issue at hand: a world is a space in which a certain tonality resonates. But that tonality is nothing other than the totality of resonances that the elements, the moments, and the places of this world echo, modulate, and modalize. This is how I can recognize a short passage from Bach or from Varese—but also a fragment from Proust, a drawing from Matisse, or a Chinese landscape.

(It can be noted, provisionally, that it is no accident that art provides the most telling examples: a world perhaps always, at least potentially, shares the unity proper to the work of art. That is, unless it is the opposite, or rather, unless the reciprocity between "world" and "art" is constitutive of both. This also concerns the Marxist's "enjoyment" of universal humanity.)

It follows from this that a world is a world only for those who inhabit it. To inhabit is necessarily to inhabit a world, that is to say, to have there much more than a place of sojourn: its place, in the strong sense of the term, as that which allows something to properly take place. To take place is to properly arrive and happen [*arriver*]; it is not to "almost" arrive and happen and it is not only "an ordinary occurrence." It is to arrive and happen as proper and to properly arrive and happen to a subject. What takes place takes place in a world and by way of that world. A world is the common place of a totality of places: of presences and dispositions for possible events.

Presence and disposition: sojourn and comportment, these are the senses of the two Greek words *ēthos* and *ethos*, which contaminate each other in the motif of a stand, a "self-standing" that is at the root of all ethics. In a different manner yet oddly analogous, the Latin terms *habitare* and *habitus* come from the same *habere*, which means first "standing" and "self-standing," to occupy a place, and from this to possess and to have (*habitudo* had meant a "manner of relating to . . ."). It is a having with a sense of being: it is a manner of being there and of standing in it. A world is an ethos, a *habitus* and an inhabiting: it is what holds to itself and in itself, following to its proper mode. It is a network of the self-reference of this stance. In this way it resembles a subject—and in a way, without a doubt, what is called a subject is each time by itself a world. But the measure or the manner of a world is not that of a subject if the latter must presuppose itself as substance or as prior support of its self-reference. The world does not presuppose itself: it is only coextensive to its extension as world, to the spacing of its places between which its resonances reverberate. (If a subject supposes itself, it subjects itself to its supposition. It can thus only presuppose itself as not subjected to any supposition. It is still, no doubt, a presupposition: thus, precisely, we can say as well that the world presupposes itself as not subjected to anything other, and that is the destiny of the so-called "modern" world. We could thus say that it presupposes itself only, but necessarily, as its own *revolution*: the way it turns on itself and/or turns against itself.)

Thus, the meaning of the world does not occur as a reference to something external to the world. It seems that meaning always refers to something other than what it is a matter of giving a meaning to (as the meaning [*sens*][15] of the knife is in the cutting and not in the knife). But thought in terms of a world, meaning refers to nothing other than to the possibility of the meaning of this world, to the proper mode of its stance [*tenue*] insofar as it circulates between all those who stand in it [*s'y tiennent*], each time singular and singularly sharing a same possibility that none of them, any place or any God outside of this world, accomplishes.

The stance of a world is the experience it makes of itself. Experience (the *experiri*) consists in traversing to the end: a world is traversed from one edge to the other, and nothing else. It never crosses over these edges to occupy a place overlooking itself. Time has passed since one was able to represent the figure of a *cosmotheoros*, an observer of a world. And if this time has passed, it is because the world is no longer conceived of as a representation. A representation of the world, a worldview, means the assigning of a principle and an end to the world. This amounts to saying that a worldview is indeed the end of the world as viewed, digested, absorbed, and dissolved in this vision. The Nazi *Weltanschauung* attempted to answer to absence of a *cosmotheoros*. And this is also why Heidegger in 1938, turning against this Nazism, exposed the end of the age of the *Weltbilder*—images or pictures of the world.[16]

The world is thus outside representation, outside its representation and of a world of representation, and this is how, no doubt, one reaches the most contemporary determination of the world. Already with Marx, there was an exit from representation that was prescribed by the world as the unfolding of a production of men by themselves (even if, with Marx, this production retains features of representation).

A world outside of representation is above all a world without a God capable of being the subject of its representation (and thus of its fabrication, of its maintenance and destination). But already, as I indicated, the God of metaphysics merged into a world. More precisely, the "God" of onto-theology was progressively stripped of the divine attributes of an independent existence and only retained those of the existence of the world considered in its immanence, that is to say, also in the undecidable amphibology of an existence as necessary as it is contingent. Let us recall, for instance, Spinoza's God, the "immanent cause of the world," or Leibniz's God, which created "the best of all possible worlds," that is to say, was limited to being a reason internal to the general order of things. The God of onto-theology has produced itself (or deconstructed itself) as subject of the world, that is, as world-subject. In so doing, it suppressed itself as God-Supreme-Being and transformed itself, losing itself therein, in the existence for-itself of the world without an outside (neither outside of the world nor a world from the outside). The speculative *Weltgeist* mocked by Marx becomes—and becomes with Marx himself—*Welt-Geist* or *Geist-Welt*: no longer "spirit of world" but rather world-spirit or spirit-world.

From this very fact, the existence of the world was at stake as absolute existence: its necessity or its contingency, its totality or incompleteness, became the inadequate terms of a problem, a problem that God's disappearance transformed completely. Correlatively, being "in" [*dans*] the world could no longer follow a container topology, any more than the world itself was found "within" something other than itself. This is how being-within-the-world [*être-dans-le-monde*] has become being-in-the-world [*être-au-monde*]. This preposition *au* [in] represents, in French, what encapsulates the problem of the world.

To be more precise, one should add: "world-forming" [*mondialisation*] was preceded by a "world-becoming" [*mondanisation*]. This means that the "worldly" world of Christianity, the world as created and fallen, removed from salvation and called to self-transfiguration, had to become the site of being and/or beings as a whole, reducing the other world therein. But, as we will see, it is from the feature of "creation" that an inscription is thus transmitted to the global world—while the internal demand of a transfiguration is transferred to the "worldly" world. For the moment, we could say: world-becoming engages a displacement of value, and world-forming a displacement of production. But neither aspect of the process is a mere "secularization" of the theological: it is complete displacement of the stakes. The world does not replay the roles of the theological script for its own purpose: it displaces everything in another script, which precisely lacks a scene that is given or laid out in advance.[17]

This brief metaphysical excursus only has a very specific function here: that of showing that "the world," in our philosophical tradition, has come to be identified firstly with the totality of beings that longer refers logically to any other being (to no other world: for a God distinct from the world would be another world), and secondly, identified with the question, enigma or the mystery of the *raison d'être* of such a totality. If it is necessary without being the effect of a superior reason (or will), what is that necessity? But if it is not necessitated by anything, isn't it then contingent?—and in this case where does the fortuitous errancy of this existence go?

And if our world is neither necessary nor contingent, or if it is both at once, what does that mean? More generally, how does one disentangle oneself from this conceptual couple? Perhaps by considering a fact without referring it to a cause (neither efficient nor final). The world is such a fact: it may well be that it is the only fact of this kind (if it is the case that the other facts take place within the world). It is a fact without reason or end, and it is our fact. To think it, is to think this factuality, which implies not referring it to a meaning capable of appropriating it, but to placing in it, in its truth as a fact, all possible meaning.

Marx's text cited earlier can be replaced within the horizon of this problematics in several ways. It is first possible to see in these lines the reflection of a sort of inverted onto-theology, where the immanent cause of a world existing in itself eternally (like the matter of/from which it is made: one should look here at Marx's studies on Epicurean materialism) is the production of humanity itself represented as the final and total accomplishment of self-production (total man would almost be the accomplished self-production of matter as the condition and force of production). But it is also possible—and it is even in some respect necessary—to interpret it differently: indeed, if the production of total humanity—that is, global humanity, or the production of the humanized world—is nothing other than the production of the "sphere of freedom," a freedom that has no other exercise than the "enjoyment of the multimorphic production of the entire world," then this final production determines no genuine end, nor *telos* or *eschaton*. It is indeed not determined by the self-conception of humanity and of world, but rather by a beyond of production itself, here named "enjoyment."

Enjoyment—in whatever way one wants to understand it, and whether one stresses a sexual connotation (by borrowing from a Lacanian problematic of the "real," if you will, something I do not want to explore further here) or by stressing the Spinozist's joy, or mystical "union" (are these two senses that different? It is not certain . . .)—enjoyment, therefore, is what (if it "is" and if it is "something")[18] maintains itself beyond either having or being in the same way that it unfolds beyond or before activity and passivity.

By identifying this enjoyment of the global production of humanity, Marx indicates an excess with respect to production as well as with respect to possession (and this is perhaps that very thing which he tried to call later "individual property," once again, neither private nor collective). Note—a troubling circumstance—that such an excess of enjoyment (and enjoyment is excessive or it is not enjoyment) constitutes something like the exact parallel of profit that is the law of capital, but a parallel that inverts the sign of surplus-production. This is the case in the sense that the extortion of surplus-value profits from the value created by the work to deposit it in the account of the accumulation in general equivalency (according to the law of an indefinite addition, the principle of which is also excessive, but an excess whose *raison d'être* is accumulation, the end/goal being to indefinitely reproduce the cycle of production and alienation). In that sense enjoyment would be shared appropriation—or appropriating sharing—of what cannot be accumulated or what is not equivalent, that is, of value itself (or of meaning) in the singularity of its creation. But sharing singularity (always plural) means to configure a world, a quantity of possible worlds in the world. This configuration (features, tones, modes, contacts, etc.) allows the singularities to expose themselves.

The extortion or the exposition of each to the others: the most important is not to say, "Here is the decisive alternative!" (which we already know). What matters is to be able to think how the proximity of the two "ex-," or this twofold excess is produced, how the same world is divided in this way.

In a way, profit and enjoyment thus placed back to back behave like two sides of the infinite: on the one hand, the infinite that Hegel called "bad," the infinite of the interminable growth of accumulation, the cycle of investment, of exploitation and reinvestment (one could say that it is the cycle of infinite wealth as it began when the world, becoming precapitalistic, came out of the order in which wealth was accumulated for its shine rather than for its reproduction),[19] on the other hand the actual infinite, the one by which a finite existence accedes, as finite, to the infinite of a meaning or of a value that is its most proper meaning and value.

I do not at all find it unreasonable to say that this perspective, which can seem perfectly abstract or idealistic, distant from harsh reality, is precisely what would be capable of diagnosing that which secretly drives our world insofar as it seems surrendered to an infinitely unruly unleashing of appetites of enjoyment: some moved by the drive of exponential accumulation, others provoked by the strategies of production that are subjugated to this drive. Under the unruly unleashing of the bad infinite (an unruly unleashing rightly called "deregulation" in free-market thinking!) that regulates itself according to the indefinite as such, there is a secret desire for the actual infinite: a desire for absolute value. Now it is manifest—it is even what current times render each day more manifest—that no abstract value, no equivalence nor any given representation of human beings or of world (or of another world), can satisfy this expectation. One does not enjoy the human being of humanism, or, if you prefer, the human being of humanism does not have joy: it is *par excellence* the human without joy, it does not even know tragic joy (let us say, in one word, the joy of knowing oneself to be finite) and it knows neither the mystical joy (that of effusion) nor the Spinozist and Nietzschean joy (let us say, the one of knowing oneself *hic et nunc* infinite and eternal).

How can this be considered in an actual relation with the world, or rather with what happens to us as a dissipation of the world in the bad infinite of a "globalization" in a centrifugal spiral behaving like the expanding universe described by astrophysics, all the while doing nothing else than circumscribing the earth more and more in a horizon without opening or exit? How are we to conceive of, precisely, a world where we only find a globe, an astral universe, or an earth without sky (or, to cite Rimbaud and reversing him, a sea without a sun)?

It at least supposes one founding condition. This condition is nothing else than the following: it is a matter of being able to take completely and seriously into account the determination of *world*, in a way that has perhaps never taken place in our history—but for which our history today would offer the possibility.

If the world, essentially, is not the representation of a universe (*cosmos*) nor that of a here below (a humiliated world, if not condemned by Christianity), but the excess—beyond any representation of an *ethos* or of a *habitus*—of a stance by which the world stands by itself, configures itself, and exposes itself in itself, relates to itself without referring to any given principle or to any determined end, then one must address the principle of such an absence of principle directly. This must be named the "without-reason" of the world, or its absence of ground. It is not a new idea to say that the world is "without reason" or that it is exclusively and entirely its own reason. We know quite well that it is found in Angelus Silesius ("the rose grows without reason"), but one does not always notice how it works within all the great formulations of the most classical rationalism, including and especially when they are trying to find and posit a "principle of reason" for all things.[20]

If I say that this thought works within the consciousness and the unconscious of the West, I mean that it is indeed an actual work, transformative and productive of value—a value that capital is not able, in spite of everything, to commodify without remainder: the value of the world, or more precisely the value of "world," the value of being-world and of being-in-the-world as significance or as a resonance without reason.

But if capital is not able to absorb all significance in the commodity, although it aims at nothing other, that is perhaps also because it does not entirely come from the commodity alone: what precedes capital is wealth as glitter, the wealth that does not produce more wealth, but which produces its own splendor and its own opulence as the glow of a meaning in which the world is wrapped (but also blinded and suffocated by its glitter—at the same time that such glitter is captured by the hierarchy). Capital converts the glitter into an accumulation that produces a wealth that is defined by its own (re)productivity: in this way, it transforms the brilliance into the indefinite process of a meaning that is always to come or always lost, and synonymous with enrichment. One could say that wealth loses in power of meaning what it gains as power of accumulation. One should never forget that the word *wealth* originally designated the order of power and greatness, the order of magnificence in the noble sense of the term:[21] the so-called grandeur of the soul, perhaps its glory and exaltation. One can also recall that it is no accident if the signs of this spiritual greatness, in the beginnings of the proto-capitalist West, shift from wealth to Christian or philosophical poverty.

In this inversion of signs and in the henceforth interminably ambivalent relation that the West maintains with money (and commerce, finance, etc.), it is not only the beginning of the capitalist transformation of society that is at stake. It is also the more secret, and tricky movement by which, in capital, a change in the nature of "wealth" is accompanied by placing grandeur in reserve (in secret), that is, by placing *value* in the "valorous" sense of the word. Value becomes both the remainder and the excess of capital, or the foreign body that weakens and undermines it from within, as the other of its "political economy," like the super-economy or an-economy that must reveal its gap and its violent demand there. It is that absolute value of value,[22] and nothing else, that erupts anew in Marx's work.

(But this is also why, far from submitting history, culture and the humanity of human beings to an economic causality, and "superstructure" to "infrastructure," Marx analyzes, on the contrary, the way in which the transformations of value—that is to say, the transformations of the evaluation of value (or of sense, or of truth)—make economic and social transformations possible, etc. In the transformations of the evaluation of value, which are the transformations of the production of the ways of life, the technological and cultural processes are inextricably joined and in reciprocal relation. Marx did not reverse the supposed "Hegelian" history from an ideal determination to a material determination: he suppressed all determinations except that of the production of humanity by itself, a production that is itself precisely determined by nothing other.)

Today, wealth as a quantity that can be capitalized is identical to the infinite poverty of the calculable quantities of the market. But that same market also produces a growing order of symbolic wealth—wealth of knowledge and significance such as those which, despite their submission to commodities, made the greatest culture of modern times, and such as those which seem to be invented today as a giant productivity that disseminates sense (symbols, signs, modes, schemes, rhythms, figures, sketches, codes for all gains and losses, in all senses, if I may say so). It could well be that capital—and perhaps its own capital, its head and reserve, the primitive accumulation of its own sense—appears in its insignificance and disseminates in a novel significance, violently disseminating all signification in order to demand the forcing or breaching of a sense yet to be invented: the sense of a world that would become rich from itself, without any reason either sacred or cumulative.

Thus, we propose a hypothesis with respect to an internal displacement of technology and capital that would make an inversion of signs possible: the insignificant equivalence reversed into an egalitarian, singular, and common significance. The "production of value" becomes the "creation of meaning." This hypothesis is fragile, but perhaps it is a matter of grasping it, not as an attempt at a description, but as a will to act. However, such an inversion of signs would not remain a simple formal inversion, if the "signs" were the indexes of an evaluation: it would be a matter of a general reevaluation, of an *Umwertung* on which Marx and Nietzsche would finally concur. On the other hand, such a possibility must not be the object of a programmatic and certain calculation. Such certainty of a prediction would immediately render the *Umwertung* sterile and would predetermine its projects, its representations and, why not, its party with its operatives. . . . It must be a possibility of the impossible (according to a logic used often by Derrida), it must know itself as such, that is to say, know that it happens also in the incalculable and the unassignable. This does not mean that the possibility of the impossible remains formal or constitutes a transcendental with no relevance to any experience. It must devote itself to being actual, but the aim of actuality must take into account, at the same time, a boundless leap outside of the calculable and controllable reality. After all, the transcendental is also, always, that which constitutes conditions of possibility of experience, while at the same time *rendering impossible the subject of that experience* as itself an empirical subject. Willing the world, but not willing a subject of the world (neither substance nor author nor master), is the only way to escape the un-world. And the materialism of actuality—of the concrete life of human beings—must here conceive of matter as impenetrable, namely as the impenetrability of the truth of the world, the "meaning of the world" being the passion of this truth.

It would thus be a matter of producing and/or of allowing for a wealth to be given that would be enriched only by the splendor of such a meaning and that, in this way, would also be "poverty," if this word does indeed designate since the beginning of the West—not by accident—not the misery resulting from spoliation, but the *ethos* (and also the *pathos*), the value of which does not derive from ownership (of something or of oneself) but in abandonment. Poverty, or the being-abandoned—in all the complex ambivalence of these two senses: abandoned *by* and abandoned *to*. (One could show the emergence of a triple figure of poverty in this sense: philosophical-Greek, Jewish, or Roman.)

The three aspects of wealth would be: glitter, capital, dissemination, and they would constitute three moments of the body: the glorious and hieratic body of the Gods, the working body subjugated to the speculative spirit, the body exposed to contact with all bodies: a world of bodies, a world of senses, a world of being-*in*-the-world. But it goes without saying that these moments do not simply succeed each other like so many stages of a process, or like the ages of the world. It is their coexistence and their conflict that needs to be thought.

What is most troubling about the modern enigma—for specifically this is what constitutes the modern and which makes it, for the last three centuries, an enigma for itself, which even defines the modern as such an enigma, without any need to speak of the "postmodern"—is that the without-reason could take the form both of capital and of the mystical rose that represents the absolute value of the "without-reason." One could almost be tempted, even beyond the wildest imaginations of today's free market capitalists, to present the rose as the ultimate revelation of the secret of capital—a revelation that projected, it is true, until the indefinable end of perpetual reinvestment. Others would be tempted—and we all are today, more or less—to reveal, on the contrary, that the secret of the rose and of capital together occurs like an unprecedented geopolitical, economic, and ecological catastrophe, globalization as the suppression of all world-forming of the world.

It is in all respects not only reasonable, but also required by the vigor and rigor of thought, to avoid recourse to representations: the future is precisely what exceeds representation. And we have learned that we must grasp the world once more outside of representation.

Now, in order to distance such thinking of the world from representation, there is no better way than this one: to grasp the "world" once more according to one of its constant motifs in the Western tradition—to the extent that it is also the tradition of monotheism—namely, the motif of creation.

To appropriate this motif, I must take a preliminary precaution, but in an elliptical manner. "Creation" is a motif, or a concept, that we must grasp outside of its theological context. Let me indicate how this can be done schematically: as I have previously suggested, it is theology itself that has stripped itself of a God distinct from the world. At the end of monotheism, there is world without God, that is to say, without another world, but we still need to reflect on what this means, for we know nothing of it, no truth, neither "theistic" nor "atheistic"—let us say, provisionally, as an initial attempt, that it is *absentheistic*.[23]

If "creation" means anything, it is the exact opposite of any form of production in the sense of a fabrication that supposes a given, a project, and a producer. The idea of creation, such as has been elaborated by the most diverse and at the same time most convergent thoughts, including the mystics of the three monotheisms but also the complex systems of all great metaphysics, is above all the idea of the *ex nihilo* (and I do not exempt Marx from this, to the contrary: while his understanding of Christian creation is only instrumental, for him value is precisely created . . .). The world is created from nothing: this does not mean fabricated with nothing by a particularly ingenious producer. It means instead that it is not fabricated, produced by no producer, and not even coming out of nothing (like a miraculous apparition), but in a quite strict manner and more challenging for thought: the nothing itself, if one can speak in this way, or rather *nothing* growing [*croissant*] as *something* (I say "growing" for it is the sense of *cresco*—to be born, to grow—from which comes *creo*: to make something merge and cultivate a growth). In creation, a growth grows from nothing and this nothing takes care of itself, cultivates its growth.

The *ex nihilo* is the genuine formulation of a radical materialism, that is to say, precisely, without roots.

Thus, we can now clarify what we said earlier: if the world-becoming (detheologization) displaces value—makes it immanent—before world-forming displaces the production of value—making it universal—the two together displace "creation" into the "without-reason" of the world. And this displacement is not a transposition, a "secularization" of the onto-theological or metaphysical-Christian scheme: it is, rather, its deconstruction and emptying out, and it opens onto another space—of place and of risk—which we have just begun to enter.

If the world is the growth of/from nothing [*croissance de rien*]—an expression of a formidable ambiguity—it is because it only depends on itself, while this "self" is given from nowhere but from itself. But it is also because it is the growth of/from nothing other than nothing, a nothing that obviously is not a pure and simple nothingness, on the basis of which no growth could be conceived, but which is the without-reason [*rien de raison*] of the world. In this sense, the "creation" of the world is in no way a representation that is opposed to the representation of an eternity of the matter of the world. In truth, none of these things, creation or eternal matter, are representations, and this is why they are not opposites. The eternity of matter only means that there is nothing outside the world, no other world, and no space-time that would not be that of "our" world. This eternity is the eternity of space-time, absolutely. Creation is the growth without reason of such a space-time. The two concepts correspond to each other at the exact limit of metaphysics and physics: and this limit is not one that separates two worlds, but one that shares out the indefiniteness of the universe (or the indefiniteness of its expansion, as contemporary cosmology has it) and the infinity of its meaning.

By writing that "the sense of the world must lie outside the world,"[24] Wittgenstein simultaneously stated two things: that the world in itself does not constitute an immanence of meaning, but that, since there is no other world, the "outside" of the world must be open "within it"—but open in a way that no other world could be posited there. This is also why Wittgenstein writes further: "It is not *how* things are in the world that is mystical, but *that* it exists" (TLP 6.44, 88).

The meaning of this *fact* is the meaning that the without-reason makes possible. Now, this means that it is meaning in the strongest and most active sense of the term: not a given signification (such as that of a creating God or that of an accomplished humanity), but meaning, absolutely, as possibility of transmission from one place to another, from the one who sends to the one who receives, and from one element to another, a reference that forms at the same time a direction, an address, a value, or a meaningful content. Such a content constitutes the stance of a world: its *ethos* and its *habitus*. Clearly, neither meaning as direction [*sens*] nor meaning [*sens*] as content is given. They are to be invented each time: we might as well say to be created, that is, to create from nothing and to bring forth that very without-reason that sustains, drives, and forms the statements that are genuinely creative of meaning, such as in science, politics, esthetics, and ethics: on all these registers, we are dealing with multiple aspects and styles of what we could call the *habitus* of the meaning of the world. (I limit myself to speaking of "statements" to remain close to the sphere where we situate meaning most commonly; one should also think of gestures, actions, passions, and formalities, etc. . . . Solidarity, love, music, cybernetics are also meaning in act.)

This does not at all mean that anything makes sense in just any way: that would be precisely the capitalist version of the without-reason, which establishes the general equivalence of all forms of meaning in an infinite uniformity. It signifies on the contrary that the creation of meaning, and with it the enjoyment of sense (which is not foreign, one should note, to the enjoyment of senses) requires its forms, its inventions of forms and the forms of its exchange. Worldhood, in this regard, is the form of forms that itself demands to be created, that is not only produced in the absence of any given, but held infinitely beyond any possible given: in a sense, then, it is never inscribed in a representation, and nonetheless always at work and in circulation in the forms that are being invented.

One could say that worldhood is the *symbolization* of the world, the way in which the world symbolizes in itself with itself, in which it articulates itself by making a circulation of meaning possible without reference to another world.

Our task today is nothing less than the task of creating a form or a symbolization of the world. This seems to us to be the greatest risk that humanity has had to confront. But it may well be that it has already done so several times, perhaps even that the world itself has already done so several times. This is neither an abstract nor purely a formal task—whether this word is taken esthetically or logically. It is the extremely concrete and determined task—a task that can only be a struggle—of posing the following question to each gesture, each conduct, each *habitus* and each *ethos*: How do you engage the world? How do you involve yourself with the enjoyment of the world as such, and not with the appropriation of a quantity of equivalence? How do you give form to a difference of values that would not be a difference of wealth in terms of general equivalence, but rather a difference of singularities in which alone the passage of a meaning in general and the putting into play of what we call a world can take place?

However, as I mentioned, this task is a struggle. In a sense, it is a struggle of the West against itself, of capital against itself. It is a struggle between two infinites, or between extortion and exposition. It is the struggle of thought, very precisely concrete and demanding, in which we are engaged by the disappearance of our representations of the abolishing or overcoming of capital. It demands that we open or discern in capital another type or another kind of a flaw than what we understood to be insurmountable contradictions, and that capital was able to overcome, thus overcoming also our representations. We must consider capital in terms of its height and power—in terms of its "wealth" and "fortune."

The moment has come to expose capital to the absence of reason, for which capital provides the fullest development: and this moment comes from capital itself, but it is no longer a moment of a "crisis" that can be solved in the course of the process. It is a different kind of moment to which we must give thought.

But such thinking is not only theoretical: now as in the past, it is practically manifest and necessary—in the sense of the necessity and manifestedness of the world—that the struggle is straightaway and definitively a matter of concrete equality and actual justice. In this sense, Marx's demand is not obsolete. The "thinking" of which we are speaking is necessarily involved both in the questioning of the "sense of the world"[25] and in immediate, political, economic, and symbolic acts. But the difference between Marx's revolution and the one in which we are perhaps underway without our knowledge—and of which a thousand revolts, a thousand rages, a thousand creations of signs are the flashing indicators—could be sketched provisionally in the following way: by conceiving of itself as a reversal of the relation of production, Marx's revolution presupposed that this reversal was equivalent to a conversion of the meaning of production (and the restitution of created value to its creator). What we have begun to learn is that it is also a matter of creating the meaning or the value of the reversal itself. Only perhaps this creation will have the power of the reversal.

Further, when Marx wrote that philosophers contented themselves with interpreting the world, and that it was henceforth a matter of changing it, he specified nothing with respect to the relations that the transformation entertains with the prevailing interpretations: Do the former suspend the latter? Do the latter determine, on the contrary, the former? Or else isn't it a matter of transforming the relation between them, and of understanding (that is to say, of enacting) that meaning is always in *praxis*, although no practice is limited to enacting a theory and although no theory is able to diminish practice? But the gap between the two is necessary to what is called *praxis*, that is to say, *meaning at work* [au travail], or even *truth in the work* [à l'œuvre].[26]

This gap is not the gap between an interpretive philosophy and a transformative action, nor is it the gap between a regulative utopia and a resigned practice, nor the gap between a founding myth and the violence that sought to incarnate it. Indeed, under the three figures—interpretation, utopia, or myth—beneath their differences, the possibility of a correspondence of truth to a form, or of a coming into presence of an accomplished meaning remains presupposed. But the issue, on the contrary, is to be attentive to the gap of meaning with itself, a gap that constitutes it or that is its truth. Such a gap always places meaning in excess or in deficiency with respect to its own work.

In excess or in deficiency with respect to its work does not mean outside of all labor, but means a labor whose principle is not determined by a goal of mastery (domination, usefulness, appropriation), but exceeds all submission to an end—that is, also exposes itself to remaining without end. Here it is art that indicates the stakes: the work of art is always also a meaning at work beyond the work [à l'oeuvre au-delà de l'œuvre], as well as a work working and opening beyond any meaning that is either given or to be given. But the opening without finality is never a work nor any product: it is the enjoyment of which Marx spoke, as enjoyment by human beings of what opens their humanity beyond all humanism. (This work is not without labor, any more than this enjoyment is without suffering.)

To create the world means: immediately, without delay, reopening each possible struggle for a world, that is, for what must form the contrary of a global injustice against the background of general equivalence. But this means to conduct this struggle precisely in the name of the fact that this *world* is coming out of nothing, that there is nothing before it and that it is without models, without principle and without given end, and that it is precisely *what* forms the justice and the meaning of a world.

Once again, to create as a struggle, which while struggling—consequently, by seeking power, by finding forces—does not seek the exercise of power—nor property—whether collective or individual, but seeks itself and its agitation, itself and the effervescence of its thought in act, itself and its creation of forms and signs, itself and its contagious communication as propagation of an enjoyment that, in turn, would not be a satisfaction acquired in a signification of the world, but the insatiable and infinitely finite exercise that is the being in act of meaning brought forth in the world [*mis au monde*].

II

Of Creation

1

The text that begins here, and which first was given as an homage to Lyotard, links up with the exchange that took place with him twenty years ago.[1] At the time, the issue was a question of judgment, and more precisely: a judgment about ends, consequently the secret or explicit decision that necessarily subtends a philosophical gesture, and which constitutes its *ethos*, the decision about what matters—for example "*a world*," a world "worthy of the name"—cannot be a choice between possibilities, but only and each time a decision about what is neither real nor possible: a decision about what is in no way given in advance, but which constitutes the eruption of the new, that is unpredictable because it is without face, and thus the "beginning of a series of appearances" by which Kant defines freedom in its relation to the world.

Such a decision is about the neither-real-nor-possible, thus, neither given nor representable, but in some way necessary and imperious (like Kantian freedom in its relation to the law that it is itself), and consequently it is a violent decision without appeal, for it decides [*tranche*] between all and nothing—or more exactly it makes some thing be in place of nothing [*elle fait être quelque chose au lieu de rien*], and this some thing is everything, for freedom cannot be divided, as Kant knew as well, neither freedom nor its object or effect. The judgment about ends or about the end, about a destination, or about a meaning of the world, is the engagement of a philosophy (*or* about what one calls a "life") ever since an end is not given: this is the birth certificate of philosophy and of our so-called "Western" or "modern" history. In this sense, it is the certificate of a day of wrath in which the tension and the decisiveness of a (first, last) judgment are unleashed, a judgment that only depends on itself. This is the *dies irae* of which Lyotard speaks in his *The Confession of Augustine*[2] and in terms of Augustine and Isaïe, as the day in which the heavens will be enveloped as in a *volumen*, folded upon the light of signs and opening to the dark opacity before creation or after its annihilation, or even withdrawn from the world as the precise moment and place of its creation and decision: space-time outside of space and time. And thus also *dies illa*: that day, that illustrious day, most remarkable because it is removed from all days, the day of end as the day of infinity.

We should derive the following from Lyotard's interest in what Kant calls "reflective" judgment, a judgment for which "the universal is not given"— Kant's proposition for what exceeds the limits of the mathematico-physical object of "determinant" judgment and of the transcendental schematism, which becomes for Lyotard the general proposition of "post-modernity": if the universal is not given, this does not mean that it needs to be dreamt or "mimicked" (the weak version of the philosophy of the "as if," a more or less latent formulation of so-called "value" philosophies), it means that it is to be invented. In other words, it seems important not to simply pose a "judgment without criteria" (another expression from Lyotard), itself defined as a judgment "maximizing concepts outside of any knowledge of reality" (and thus in the first place the concept of final end or of destination of the world and of human beings). But one needs to understand also that knowledge is lacking here, not because of an intrinsic deficiency of human understanding (a finitude relative to the model of an *intellectus intuitivus*) but because of the absence, pure and simple, of "reality," which is effectively not given (the absolute finitude of a Dasein who puts into play nothing less than the—infinite—meaning of being).

In other words, the judgment without criteria is not only (or perhaps not at all) an analogical and approximate, symbolic and nonschematic mode of determinant judgment. It is neither its extension, nor its projection, nor its figuration. Perhaps even, in the end, the term *judgment* contains an ambiguity in its false symmetry or its apparent continuity. For whereas the first proceeds by construction, or schematic presentation, that is to say by the dependence of a concept on an intuition, which defines the conditions of a *possible* experience, the second is placed before—or provoked by—something that cannot be constructed, which corresponds to an absence of intuition. This absence of intuition forms the Kantian condition of the "absolute" object, the one that cannot be an object, that is, the subject of principles and ends ("God," or now man, in any case the rational subject, which becomes the precise term of the nonintuitable subject of sufficient reasons and final ends). The inconstructible of an absence of intuition—which moreover *produces* an absence of concept if those of "first cause" and "final end" are thereby weakened in their very structure— defines the necessity, not of constructing in the void (which has no meaning, except by simulacrum) but of letting a void emerge, or to make with this void what is at issue, namely *the end*, which is henceforth the issue of such a *praxis* rather than a strictly intellectual judgment.

To say it in a word: not to construct but to create.

(Here I allow myself a brief digression: to encounter the *inconstructible* in the Kantian sense, this is also and at the very least is what "to deconstruct" means, a word that is now too often used by the *doxa* to mean demolition and nihilism. Yet, through Husserl, Heidegger, and Derrida, this word—originally *Abbau* and not *Zerstörung*—would have rather led us toward what is neither constructed nor constructible, but is set back from the structure, its empty space, and which makes it work, or even that which pervades it.

Lyotard stated at that time that the judgment about ends should be freed from Kant's unitary teleology, that of the reign of a "reasonable humanity." Aware of the fact that the substitution of plurality for unity alone simply risked displacing an unchanged structure toward the renewed content that he named "the horizon of a manifold or of a diversity," he rushed to add that the *final* plurality imposed with it the irreducibility of singularities—which he understood in the sense of the Wittgenstein's "language games"—and that the universal coming to supplement a "non given" universal could only be the prescription of "observing the singular justice of each game."

In other words, what is necessary is a world that would only be the world of singularities, without their plurality constructed as a unitotality. But what is thus necessary is *a world*.

An exigency appears here that will have constantly—we can be certain of it—inhabited our thoughts and that always accompanies in various ways a concern that in the end is common to our absence of community, perhaps to our refusal of community and of a communitarian destination: how to do justice, not only to the whole of existence, but to all existences, taken together but distinctly and in a discontinuous way, not as the totality of their differences, and differends—precisely not that—but as these differences together, coexisting or co-appearing, held together as multiple—and thus together in a multiple way, if one can put it this way, or as multiple together, if we can state it even less adequately . . .—and held by a *co-* that is not a principle, or that is a principle or archi-principle of spacing in the principle itself. (Twenty-five years ago, Lyotard already wrote: "We would love multiplicities of *principles* . . .")[3]

To do justice to the multiplicity and to the coexistence of singularities, to multiply thus, and infinitely singularize the ends, such is one of the concerns left to us by that time which as "post" could well be a first time, a time suspended in the preexistence of another time, another beginning and another end.

Justice rendered to the singular plural is not simply a demultiplied or diffracted justice. It is not a unique justice interpreted according to perspectives or subjectivities—and nonetheless it remains the same justice, equal for all although irreducible and insubstitutable from one to the other. (One of the secrets or one of the most powerful resources held in history for the last two centuries, or since Christianity is hidden here: the equality of persons in the incommensurability of singularities.) This justice is thus, to take up a theme that is also found in Augustine's *Confessions*, without common measure: but its incommensurability is indeed the only unit with which we will have to measure the judgment about ends. This implies two conjoined considerations: on the one hand, the end or the ends will be incommensurable to any determinant aim of a goal, of an objective, of any accomplishment, and on the other hand, human "community" (perhaps also the being-together of all beings) will have no other common measure than that excess of the incommensurable. In other words, what Kant called "reasonable humanity," instead of being the tangential approximation of a given rationality (as, for instance, in utopias and their models of mechanical equilibrium), or instead of simply consisting in the conversion of this postulated unity into a diffraction of singularities, will have to conceive of its own rationality as the incommensurability of Reason in itself, or to itself.

Such a judgment about ends can neither be simply defined as a manner of extrapolation from the determinant judgment nor as an extension of concepts outside of the conditions of knowledge, under the Kantian condition of a "solely reflective" usage. At this point, it becomes no doubt necessary to think that whereas Kant understands this usage according to a strategic prudence toward the metaphysical *Schwärmerei*, we must think it also in terms of an active and productive invention of ends. We could also formulate this as follows: the Kantian order of *postulation* instead of constituting a simple supplement of representation to the harshness of the moral law that is superimposed on a finite knowledge, must constitute by itself the *praxis* of the relation to ends.

We can therefore think that the "maximization of concepts" of which Lyotard spoke must be taken beyond itself, while at the same time taken literally: the *maximum* carried to the extreme, but here precisely the extreme is not determinable and the *maximum* behaves like an infinite extension or an excess. In the movement of this excess, the "concept" that was "maximized" wavers and changes its nature or status: this is how the judgment of the sublime behaves when "the concept of the large number is transformed into the Idea of an absolute or actual infinite."[4]

The "Idea," to use this Kantian-Lyotardian lexicon, is no longer a concept used in an analogical or symbolic mode outside of the limits of possible experience or of given intuition. It is no longer a concept without intuition, handled by virtue of something that substitutes for a sensible given: it becomes itself the creation of its own scheme, that is to say, of a novel reality, which is the form/matter of a world of ends. At the same time, and according to the requirements mentioned beforehand, this scheme must be that of a multiple universal, namely, the scheme of a differend or of a general or absolute incommensurability.

(In parentheses, we shall note the following: the schematism of such a world of ends could very well correspond to what Kant calls "nature." Indeed,

if the concern of the first *Critique* is the reduction of the natural sensible multiplicity in favor of an objectivity of experience, the concern of the third *Critique* is to do justice, in a reflective mode, to that sensible excess with respect
to the object that is constituted by the vertiginous and irreducible proliferation of the "empirical laws" of nature. Now, this proliferation, where the
understanding risks losing itself, corresponds to nothing else than to the question of ends: To what end is there such a multiplicity of empirical principles?
[A question that is specified especially in these: To what end the "formative
force" of life? And to what end the production and progress of human culture?] *Nature*, with Kant, no longer constitutes a given order and becomes the
order—or always possible disorder—of an enigma of ends. Between the first
and the third *Critique*, the second will have formed the moral judgment—a
judgment concerning action regulated by a formal universality—according to
what could not for Kant have the constituting or constructive nature of a
scheme, but which, under the name of *type*, nonetheless presents the analogical regulation of a *nature* [the moral reign as a second nature]. Through this
entire reevaluation of nature, it is a matter of only this: How can we think the
undiscoverable unity, the motion, intention, or destination of this order of
things that carries naturally within it the nonnatural being of ends? The question of nature has thus indeed become that of a universe no longer sustained
by the creative and organizing action of a Providence, and, consequently, that
of a finality no longer guided by the agency or index of an end: neither of *one*
end nor of an *end* in general . . .)

We thus need to look for a judgment ruled by such a schematism, once
again, neither determinant (or presenting) nor reflective (or representing *as if*)
and, in other words, neither mathematical nor aesthetic (in the first sense of
term according to Kant) and consequently perhaps both ethical and aesthetic
(in the second sense of the term), but then just as much neither ethical nor aesthetic in any usual sense of these terms.

To that end, we need to start again from that with which judging is concerned: the ends, but more precisely those ends that are distinct from both the
mere absence of end (that is to say, mathematics) and the intentional end (the
technological end, that is, that of art in general, even if "without ends"—to that
extent, we need to stand outside of art itself, as art itself demands, which is
never "artistic" *in the last analysis*). Perhaps we have, then, no other concept of
"end" than those that I just mentioned, and perhaps our question engages a
rupture with any kind of end as an end that is sought after, that is, also as an
end represented and executed by the effect of this self-moving representation
(namely, in Kant the end of a *Will*) and at the same time as an end produced
from a cause and more broadly from the effect of a concourse of causes: formal

cause, efficient cause, material cause, and final cause, this last one essentially encapsulating causality per se—which, we note in passing, also means for Aristotle the Good as final end.[5] In this sense, our question is through and through the question of the Good in a world without end or without singular ends . . .

Reading Kant more closely, we can say that we find ourselves, in reality, dealing with an element already mentioned briefly, the "formative power" of nature that Kant describes[6] as possessing an "impenetrable property," and which "has nothing analogous to any causality known to us." The reflective judgment can only add to it a "distant analogy" with our technological finality and causality. (One can certainly note that Kant speaks here of life, not of nature in general. But we could show that the first holds for the second: the Kantian distinction is not between an inorganic nature and an organic nature [then, on another level, a culture], but between an order of the conditions of the understanding and an order of the expectations of reason. With respect to the second order, "nature" is from the outset entirely regulated by an "internal finality" that life exposes and that humanity brings to a paroxysm.)

Now what can clearly be seen in this "formative power" with a unique causality is that the thesis of a creation of the world is rendered inadmissible by the destitution of a God-principle of the world, but at the same time revived or made more acute by contrast by the demand to think a world whose reason and end, provenance and destination, are no longer given; and yet, we need to think of it as world, that is, as a totality of meaning, at least hypothetical or asymptotic—or as a totality of a meaning that is in itself plural and always singular.

Such an end that would exclude the intentional end, or a final cause that would include the formal cause, or substance itself, and would tend to identify with the absence of end would amount in Aristotle's thought to an empty tautology: "why a thing is itself."[7] But from the void of tautology since Kant, the reality of a new world, or a new reality of the world perhaps emerges. For the pure and simple absence of end conforms to the mathematical scheme, or to that of the constructible object. But here we are speaking of the inconstructible, that is to say, of *existence*, whose inconstructibility, indeterminacy, and nonobjectiveness ultimately constitute for Kant the definition of existence.[8]

Existence as such is precisely what cannot be presented as an object within the conditions of possible experience. As the first two "Analogies of Experience" demonstrate, the substance changes in time, but it is no more born there than it dies there. The *substantia phaenomenon* is clearly coextensive to time and space, which both form the unfolding of the phenomenon. Kant recalls the principle, *Gigni de nihilo nihil, in nihilum nil posse reverti.*[9] This principle explicitly states the negation of a creation. And it is also this principle that, while

64

maintaining the object within the conditions of possible experience, that is, as mechanism, excludes in an impossible experience any consideration of the end of things as well as the provenance of their existence as such.

Our question thus becomes clearly the question of the impossible experience or the experience of the impossible: an experience removed from the conditions of possibility of a finite knowledge, and which is nevertheless an experience. The judgment about ends without given criteria—and which makes by itself, in act, the *ethos* and *praxis* of this "finality" in all respects singular—is the "experience" in question. In a sense, philosophy after Kant was continuously the thought of an experience of the impossible, that is, an experience of the *intuitus originarius*, or the originary penetration by which there is a world, existences, their "reasons," and their "ends." The problem was as follows: *Without giving up on the strict critical delimitation of metaphysics, how can we reopen and inaugurate anew the essence of the metaphysical capacity and demands, and therefore of the discerning of reasons and ends?*

On the other hand, what is "impossible" according to the Kantian context of a delimiting "possible," tracing the circumference of the nonoriginary understanding (not creative of its object, or rather constructive of its object, but not creative of the thing, nor consequently of the provenance-and-end of the world), is also what has changed, since Descartes and especially since Leibniz, from the status of the real to the status of the possible, now understood not as delimiting, but rather as the unlimiting mode of openness and activity. The world is a possibility before being a reality, reversing the perspective from the given to the giving, from the result to the provenance (without forgetting, however, that there is no longer a giver). The "best of all possible worlds" is an expression that refers above all to the activity by which this world is drawn (or draws itself) from the immensity of possibilities.[10] The thinking that inaugurates plural monadic singularity is the one that transforms (but with Descartes and Spinoza) the regime of thought of the provenance-and-end of the world: from creation as a result of an accomplished divine action, one shifts to creation as, in sum, an unceasing activity and actuality of this world in its singularity (singularity of singularities). One sense of the word (creation as a state of affairs of the given world) yields to another (creation as bringing forth [*mise au monde*] a world—an active sense that is nothing else than the first sense of *creatio*). Hence, even the *creature* that was the finite image of its creator[11] and consequently was bound to represent (interpret, figure) creation, itself becomes a potential *creator* as subject of possibilities and subject of ends, as being of distance and of its own distance, or still (or at the same time) confronts "creation"—origin and end—as the incommensurable and impossible of its experience.

But that very fact, that there is in the world either the agency or the power or at least the question and/or experience of its own creation, is henceforth given with the world and as its very worldliness—which, from created, becomes creative—even in the end as its worldhood. The current state of affairs is that there is in the world or even *as* the world (under the name "humanity" or under other words, "history," "technology," "art," "existence") a putting into play of its provenance and end, of its being-possible and thus of its being and of being in general, and that this putting into play itself be the entire discernible necessity in place of a being necessarily situated above and beyond the world.[12]

Consequently, what indirectly appears as a new problematic of "creation" is the question of a judgment about ends that would not be only a judgment extrapolated beyond the limits of the understanding, but also, or rather, the judgment of a reason to which is given in advance neither end(s) nor means, nor anything that constitutes whatever kind of "causality known to us." The judgment about the "ends of all things" must be concerned with a condition of being that would not depend on causality or finality, nor consequently on mechanical consecution or subjective intention. By destituting the creating God and the *ens summum*—sufficient reason of the world—Kant also makes clear that the reason of the world pertains to a productive causality. He opens implicitly and outside of theology a new question of "creation" . . .

At the same time, a second guiding indication is given to us: what excludes the *ex nihilo* from the Kantian understanding is the necessary permanence of the unique phenomenal substance in which changes occur by way of causality. But the uniqueness of this substance is itself the correlation of the "principle of production" (second Analogy) of all phenomena. Now, what we have said thus far forces us to posit that the principle, not of all phenomena but of the *totality* of phenomena and of phenomenality itself, or the ontological principle of the phenomenality *of* the thing in itself, precisely cannot be a principle of production; it must be that which appears indirectly as a "creation," that is to say, a provenance without production. It is neither procession nor providence, nor project, a provenance without a *pro-*, prototype, or promoter—or else a *pro-* that is *nihil* in the very property of *pro-*venance.

Consequently, and even if we still know nothing of such a "principle of creation," it could well be that what production connects a priori as and in the uniqueness of a substance finds itself on the contrary dispersed by creation—and no less a priori—in an essential plurality of substances: in a multiplicity of existences whose singularity, each time, is precisely homologous to existence, if *existence* is indeed that which detaches itself or distinguishes itself absolutely (what stands out in *all* the senses of the expression), and not that which can be produced by something else.[13]

In this sense, an existence is necessarily a finite cut on (or in, or out of . . .) the indefinite (or infinite as interminable) permanence, in the same way that it is the nonphenomenal underneath (or in, or out of . . .) the phenomenal of the same permanence. But this finitude is precisely what constitutes the real and absolute infinite or the act of this existence: and in this infinite it engages its most proper end.

At least in two ways, conjoined and co-implicated—one that pertains to the provenance and destination of the world, and one that concerns the plurality of subjects—the Lyotardian question of a judgment about ends without given end and without teleological unity, the question of an end *ad infinitum* thus leads toward a question that it seems inevitable to call the question of "creation."

2

However, this needs to be further clarified.

First, I only use the word *creation* here in a preliminary or provisional way, reserving the hope of being able to transform it. In the end, this word cannot suffice for it is overdetermined with and overused by monotheism, although it also indicates in this entire philosophical context the wearing out [*usure*] of monotheism itself (we will return to this), and even if, furthermore, I do not know what word could replace it, unless it is not a matter of replacing it but of allowing it to be erased in the existing of existence.

Through all the significations that are associated with it, the word *creation* refers, on the one hand, to monotheistic theologies,[14] and, on the other hand, to the intellectual montage of the idea of a production from nothing, a montage so often and so vigorously denounced by the adversaries of monotheism.[15] The nothing or nothingness used as a material cause supposes in fact a prodigious efficient cause (where theology seems to yield to magic), and supposes moreover that the agent of this efficiency is itself a preexisting subject, with its representation of a final cause and of a formal cause, unless the latter preexists, for its part, which would accentuate the contradictions. Stated in this way, in effect, that is, at least according to the most ordinary theological *doxa*, "creation" is the most disastrous of concepts. (Or else it is necessary to state that the *nihil* subsumes the four causes together, and with them their subject: it only remains then, according to all appearances, a word without a concept . . .)

Further, one could show that the intrinsic difficulties of this notion have led to the most powerful and most subtle theological and philosophical elaborations in all the great classical thoughts, in particular with respect to the freedom of the creator in relation to or in its creation, or else concerning its motive or absence of motive and certainly of its intention or of its expectation (glory, power, love . . .).

However, it happens, and certainly it is no accident, that the thinkers of the three monotheisms—particularly the Jewish, Christian and Islamic mystics[16]—have developed a thinking, or perhaps we should say an experience of thought that is quite different, and that one can find in the work of Hegel and Schelling among others, and also certainly, albeit secretly, in Heidegger, but one, as I have suggested, that was first implicit in Kant. Now in this grand tradition, which is also, if one considers it full scope, a thinking of Being (of the Being of beings as a whole) on the basis of a monotheism in all of its forms and ultimate consequences (the Greek thinking of Being on the basis of which there is *logos* of Being, along with the Jewish thinking of existence on the basis of which there is an experience of existence: a blending that forms the strange "with" of our Greek-Jew condition), one will find a twofold simultaneous movement:

- On the one hand, the creator necessarily disappears in the very midst of its act, and with this disappearance a decisive episode of the entire movement that I have sometimes named the "deconstruction of Christianity"[17] occurs, a movement that is nothing but the most intrinsic and proper movement of monotheism as the integral absenting of God in the unity that reduces it in and where it dissolves;
- On the other hand, and correlatively, Being falls completely outside of any presupposed position and integrally displaces itself into a transitivity by which it is, and is only, in any existence, the infinitive of a "to exist," and the conjugation of this verb (Being is not the basis the existent, or its cause, but it "is" it or it "exists" it).

In this twofold movement, on the one hand, the model of causal production according to given ends has been clearly delineated and classified in terms of the object, representation, intention and will. On the other hand, the non-model or model-less-ness of being without given—without universal given, without agent given and without presupposed or desired ends, that is to say, without or with nothing given, without or with no gift given—has revealed its incommensurable real and will have challenged the judgment that Kant, in fact, advanced in his way, implicitly inscribing the enigma of creation.

Being without given can only be understood with the active sense of the verb "to be," indeed, a transitive sense:[18] "to be," not as a substance or as a substrate, even less as a result or product, nor as a state, nor as a property, even less, if it is possible, with a simple function of a copula. This is the case because "the world is" forms a complete proposition without the attribute of its subject, but as an act, and thus equivalent to "a doing," although not conforming to any of the known modes of "doing" (neither as a producing nor engendering nor providing a model, nor founding, in sum, a "doing" neither done nor to be done . . .). A transitive "being," whose historical senses of the terms used for the idea of "creation" only give vague approximations (*bara*, the Hebrew term reserved for that divine act, *kitzo*, the Greek term that signifies "to plant," "draw from the wild state," "to establish," the Latin term *creo*, the transitive form of *cresco* "to grow," thus "to cultivate," to "care for").[19]

This *being* is incommensurable to any given as to any operation that supposes a given put into play (and an agent-operator). Its substance is equal to its operation, but its operation does not operate any more than it lets the . . . *nothing* be or make (itself), a nothing, that is, as we know, *res*, the thing itself. This being is not nothing, it *is* (transitively) *nothing. It transits nothing into something, or rather nothing transits itself into something.*

This theme cuts short any thought of whatever would remain buried at the heart of being or at the very bottom of it. There is nothing withdrawn in the innermost depths of the origin, *nothing but the nothing of origin.* Consequently, the origin cannot be lost or lacking, the world is lacking nothing, because the being of the world is the thing permeated by the nothing. Perhaps this should be decisively separated from any thought of the phenomenon (appearance/disappearance, presence/absence), without for that matter appropriating the secret of presence "in itself": there is no longer a thing in itself or a phenomenon but rather the transitivity of being-nothing.[20] Is this not, in the end, what Nietzsche had been the first one to understand?

The withdrawal of any given thus forms the heart of a thinking of creation. This is also what distinguishes it from myth, for which, in a general manner, there is something given, something primordial and which precedes it, which constitutes precedence itself, and the provenance from it. Monotheism is no longer the regime of the foundational myth, but one of a history of election and of destination: the unique God is absolutely not the reunion or the subsumption (nor the "spiritualization") of multiple Gods under a principle (a unique principle figures very often at the foundation of the mythological world).

One needs to state the following: "polytheism" and "monotheism" are not related to each other like a multiplicity to unity. In the first case, there are Gods, that is, presences of absence (because the absolutely general law of any presence is its multiplicity). In the second case, there is atheism, or the absenting of presence. The "Gods" are no longer anything but "places" where this absenting arrives (to be born, to die, to feel, to enjoy, to suffer, to think, to begin and end).

Mono-theism or a-theism is thus a complete metamorphosis of divinity and origin. Nothing is given any longer, except that alone which is still given (for the world of myth does not completely disappear, just as the Babylonian myths of the "creation of the world" infuse the "Book of Generation" or "Book of Genesis"). It is the gift offered by the unique God, but if this gift is still given from one side (this is creation as a state, the world received by man), it cannot be reduced to that state: it is more properly giving, it is the very act of gift and in this act the singular history according to which the human being—and with it all "creatures"—is a partner more than a simple recipient of divine action (for to receive the gift is part of the gift itself) is engaged.

In its profound truth, creation is thus nothing that pertains to a production or fashioning of the ground; it is through and through the mobilization of an act and this act is that of a relation between two actors or agents, God and his creature, consequently each of them singular. Creation "makes" with "nothing," because it makes nothing that is the order of a substrate: what it "makes" is history and relation, and in this sense it is no thing nor comes from anything. It is thus not a question any longer of a "making" but of a "being," but only in the sense that *this being is nothing but the meaning of history or of the relation in which it is engaged.*

This is why the most noted mystical version of creation, that of the *tsim-tsoum* of the Lurianic kabala[21] states that the "nothing" of creation is the one that opens in God when God withdraws in it (and in sum *from* it) in the act of creating. God annihilates itself [*s'anéantit*] as a "self" or as a distinct being in order to "withdraw" in its act—which makes the opening of the world.

Creation forms, then, a nodal point in a "deconstruction of monotheism," insofar as such a deconstruction proceeds from monotheism itself, and perhaps is its most active resource. The unique God, whose unicity is the correlate of the creating act, cannot precede its creation any more that it can subsist above it or apart from it in some way. It merges with it: merging with it, it withdraws in it, and withdrawing there it empties itself there, emptying itself it is nothing other than the opening of this void. Only the opening is divine, but the divine is nothing more than the opening.

The opening is neither the foundation nor the origin. Nor is the opening any longer a sort of receptacle or an extension prior to things of the world. The opening of the world is what opens along such things and among them, that which separates them in their profuse singularity and which relates them to each other in their coexistence. The open or the "nothing" weaves the co-appearance of existences without referring them to some other originary or foundational unity. As Gérard Granel writes, "The open needs the closed or even is a mode of the closed, a concrete expression of the essential finitude that any form of being modulates . . . it is at the Closed that the Open itself opens, wounds itself, and only in this way *is* open."²² But the "finitude" in question here must, in the same movement, be understood as the end in which or toward which the open infinitely opens itself: an end indefinitely multiplied by and in every existing thing in the world. The "world" itself is only the unassignable totality of meaning of all these ends that are open between themselves and the infinite.

The world of myth, and of polytheism, is the world of given presupposition. Onto-theology—the suspension of myth—is, on the contrary, the order of posited presupposition: actively posited as the affirmation of the unique God and/or as thesis of Being. Insofar as it is not given, but posited, the presupposition also contains the principle of its own deposition, since it cannot presuppose anything like a cause (nor thus therefore like an end) or like a production, without also extending, correlatively, the limits of the world. The presupposition becomes there infinite or null, and this simple statement contains the entire program of onto-theology with respect to the ground *and* with respect to the auto-deconstruction of this ground, that is, with respect to its access to the inconstructible. In other words, if nihilism corresponds to the accomplishment of onto-theology according to the logic of a "bad" infinite of presupposition, on the other hand, a thinking of "creation" constitutes the exact reverse of nihilism, conforming to the logic of a null presupposition (which is equivalent as well to a "good" infinite, or actual infinite).

The *ex nihilo* contains nothing more, but nothing less, than the ex- of existence that is neither produced nor constructed but only *existing* [*étante*] (or, if one prefers, *étée*, "made" from the making constituted by the transitivity of being). And this *ex nihilo* fractures the deepest core of nihilism from within.

Neither given nor posited, the world is only present: the present of the present of the day in which it exists, *dies illa*. That illustrious and infinitely distant day, that day of the end and of the judgment, is also the day of all days, the *today* of each here. This presence neither differs nor is derived from any other presupposed presence, any more than from an absence that would be the negative of a presence: *ex nihilo* means that it is the *nihil* that opens and that disposes itself as the space of all presence (or even as one will see, of all *the* presences).

In a sense, this presence does differ at all (it differs from nothing and it does not differ from anything which is): the ontological difference is null, and this is certainly what the proposition, according to which Being is the Being of beings and nothing other, means. Being is: *that* the being exists. This is how, for example, Wittgenstein understands the meaning of "creation" when he says that the word describes the experience that I have when "*I wonder about the existence of the world.*"²³

71

"*That* the being is" can be understood as the *fiat* of creation. But this "that" conflates the indicative, the subjunctive, and the imperative: thus, the transitivity of the verb "to be" is modalized. The fact of being is identical to the desire for being and to the obligation of being; or being, by being, desires itself and obliges itself. But in the absence of any subject of a desire, or of an order, this means that the *fiat*—the fact of the *fiat*—erases in itself the difference of a necessity and of a contingency, as well as that of a possible and of a real. Since nothing produces the being, there is neither contingency nor necessity of its being, just as the question of the "freedom" of a "creator" disappears in the identity of freedom and of necessity required by creation *ex nihilo*. The nullity of the ontological difference is also the nullity of the difference between necessity and contingency and/or freedom or even between the "is" and the "ought" of being.

Derrida's *différance* is the articulation of the nullity of the ontological difference: it attempts to think that "being" is nothing other than the "ex" of existence. This articulation is thought as that of a self-presence that differs *itself*.[24] But the "self" resolves itself in *nihil* as soon as the presupposition is deposed (and deposes itself . . .): the itself/self [*se/soi*] is the presupposition par excellence or absolutely, and it is nothing other (it is the presupposition with its obligatory corollary, the postposition of an end, of a final cause of the *world*). The *supposed* (or the *subject*) becomes thus null or infinite: it is itself the *nihil* and the *ex-*; it is the *ex nihilo*. The entire being-to-self of the being of the world, and its presence consists in it. This presence is neither that of a given present [*Gegenwärtigkeit, Vorhandenheit*], nor that of a "self presenting." It is *praes-entia*, being—always-ahead-of-itself, *stepping out of itself ex-nihilo*. One should not understand *différance* as a sort of permanent flight of an asymptotic and unattainable self (a representation too frequent and too linked to a sort of desire exhausting itself in the infinite) but rather as the generating structure proper to the *ex nihilo*.

Nothing *presents itself*—which also means not even *a* nothing, nor *the* nothing present themselves: this is the end of negative theology as well as the end of a phenomenology in general, albeit that of the unapparent. The present does not present itself, and it is no less exposed. It is nothing other than that, and that is what it falls to us to think henceforth.

In the Being or in the presence of "creation," the infinite as nothing (infinite = no thing) passes into the finite. This is not an individuation or a singularization, it is not a process of production or of generation and it is not a dialectical mediation. The infinite *is* finite: it does not come out of itself *ad extra* it is rather hollowed "in itself" (in nothing) from its own withdrawal which also constitutes its opening in which finite singularities dispose themselves. This opening as nothing, which neither presents nor gives itself, is opened right at the same level of [*à même*] the finite singularities as their being together or their being-with, and constitutes the disposition of the world.

As its name indicates, *dis*-position is a gap, and its model is more spatial than temporal. Rather than the infinite delay of a *différance* to itself in the sense of a differing from itself, or else as finitude itself—that is to say, the absoluteness—of this delay (and *not* its finishing), it is the infinitely finite spacing of the singularities that constitute the event of Being or the event of "being." But strictly speaking, there is neither being nor event: nothing comes from nor comes forth if nothing is presupposed. There are existences, their styles, their comings and goings . . .

According to this archi-spatiality of disposition, which is also the spaciousness of the opening, what is at stake is not a provenance of Being (nor a being of provenance or of origin), but a spacing of presences. These presences are necessarily plural. They do not come from the dispersion of a presence: they are existing, but less in the sense of an ekstasis from an immanent "self" (emanation, generation, expression, etc.) than as disposed together and exposed to each other. Their *co*existence is an essential dimension of their presences at the edges of which the opening opens. The *co*- is implicated in the *ex*-: nothing exists unless *with*, since, nothing exists unless *ex nihilo*. The first feature of the creation of the world is that it creates the *with* of all things: that is to say *the world*, namely, the *nihil* as that which opens [*ouvre*] and forms [*œuvre*] the world.

Coexistence is neither given nor constructed. There is no schematizing subject and no prior gift.[25] Nor, consequently, is it "self-giving": a unique presence, without doubt, would give itself (it would amount to the same thing, perhaps, being the cause of itself, to be *causa sui* like God). But coexistence is the gift *and* the holding back just as it is the subject and the thing, presence and absence, plenitude and void. Coexistence is that which coheres without being "one" and without being sustained by anything else, or rather by being sustained by nothing: by the *nothing* of the *co*- that is indeed nothing but the in-between or the with of the being-together of singularities. That nothing-with is the non-cause of the world, material, efficient, formal, and final. This means both that the world is simply there (it is or it permeates its "there," its spacing) and that it is the coexistence that it does not contain but that on the contrary "makes" it.

That the world is there means that it is nowhere since it is the opening of space-time. That it is coexistence means that its opening opens it in all the senses, *partes extra partes*, spatio-temporal dis-positing dispersion, and between space and time just as the one in the other, a manner identical to its proper distention.[26] Such is the *Auseinandertreten* of which Heidegger speaks, and whose division or decision opens, in Heidegger's vocabulary, the belongingness to Be-ing.[27]

The separation, the stepping-out-of-one-another, is at the same time, *Entscheidung*, decision: it is to the decision of Being, the decision of nothing into being or to being, that responds, on the one hand, the disposition or the diffraction of the world that is (that makes) the world, and, on the other hand, the decision of existence by which a "subject" comes to the world. "Coming to the world" means birth and death, emerging from nothing and going to nothing, which are the relation to the world or the relation-world, the sharing of its meaning and the whole of existence as an ensemble or partition of singular decisions.

It is for us to decide for *ourselves*.

III

Creation as Denaturation: Metaphysical Technology

1

Philosophy begins from itself: this is a permanent axiom for it, which is implicit or explicit in the work of all philosophers, except, perhaps, for Marx—which remains to be determined—if we can assume Marx is indeed a philosopher, which also remains to be determined; in any case, the assertion holds, clearly, from Plato to Heidegger. Philosophy can represent to itself what precedes its own beginning as an early stage (an infancy, the very beginnings of reason), or else as simply an exteriority (a mythical world foreign to that of *logos*). In any case, this properly philosophical initiative belongs to philosophy itself. In a correlative and identical way, philosophy gives itself its own name: not only does it baptize itself, by inaugurating itself and in order to inaugurate itself, with the name *philo-sophia*, but it is philosophy itself that forges this word, the first of all the *termini technici* that it would forge in the course of history (and it tells itself the history, or the legend of this linguistic initiative).

Philosophy begins as the self-productive technology of its own name, its discourse, and its discipline. It engenders or it fabricates its own concept or its own Idea for itself at the same time that it invents or constructs these instrumental and ideal realities of the "concept" and the "Idea." In this operation, the best known and most prominent feature is the differentiation of itself from what is called "sophistry": with respect to this technology of *logos*, philosophy defines itself and constitutes itself as that *technē* that is at the same time different from any other *technē* because it speaks first, or finally, the truth about it. In that very way, it invents itself also in its difference from any other knowledge, any other discipline, or any other science. With respect to this major difference, its self-institution is the key.

In order to conceive of its own provenance, philosophy must choose one of the following alternatives: either it represents its provenance as the product of a continuous progression of humanity, or it represents it as an accident without conditions or reasons. In either case, philosophy is deficient or lacking with respect to its tasks. In the first case, it must retroactively project a scheme of growth or progress prior to the birth of philosophy that raises two difficulties:

77

first, something of philosophy must be presupposed prior to it, and in that case, philosophy would not have begun from itself; second, this scheme must also be extended ahead of it and as the scheme of both its own history and history in general, which has not failed to provoke, in the history of philosophy, well-known questions on the notion of "progress" in general (that is to say, in the final analysis concerning a supposed naturality and/or concerning its scientificity: thus concerning the constitution of its proper *technē*). But in the second case—with the thesis of the accident that considers the West to be an accident, according to the formulation so often repeated, and which can either refer to a happy accident, "the miracle of Greece," or else an unhappy accident, a metaphysical decline from the fleeting dawn of the meaning of Being, while remaining subject to the same scheme of accident and contingency—in this case philosophy fails to confer the least necessity to its *technē*, and it can furthermore not tolerate an appeal to it, in a more or less explicit manner, to a category as inconsistent and as unphilosophical as what is previously designated by the expression "the miracle of Greece." We will say that this expression is not philosophical but purely, and weakly, ideological. Still, it would be necessary to know what is meant by "ideology," that is, how we distinguish it from philosophy: this leads us back to the first formulations of the problem.

By willing itself auto-initiating and thus auto-finite or auto-finalized—and by willing itself *auto-* in a general way, in being and in only being able to be the *will of the auto-* in the two meanings of the genitive—philosophy betrays and reveals the history of a same movement, if one can, at least, try to understand by "history" in a provisional way, the reality of a movement and of a temporality that would not be split between teleological necessity and blind accidentality and closed on its own discontinuity. (Isn't the entire problem for history today to resolve this antinomy?)

Philosophy betrays history, because history, if it designates anything, designates above all nonbeginning and noncompletion by itself. If something such as a process-by-itself, speaking absolutely, is given somewhere or in some way, it excludes, in principle, any history: nothing can happen to it except its own reduction as a process into a result. (This is exactly the point around which one can debate the well-known model of "Hegelian history" indefinitely: the point is to know whether the process is absorbed in the result, or whether the result is not, rather and without reserve, the process itself without final result. One will say as much, and *a fortiori*, of a Marxist history leading to the activity of a "free labor," the production of a result as an infinite production . . .)

History is the order of what locates the origin and the end elsewhere, in another time—that is to say, in time itself, since it is nothing but the alterity and the alteration of the same, or of the same altering itself. History is not "nature," if "nature" has its origin and end in itself (supposing that nature exists or rather that it *still* exists in a *history* that precisely locates elsewhere, without end, the very naturality of any nature: as if that history included henceforth the *natura naturans* of any *natura naturata* and, consequently also its *natura denaturans*). History is the infinite deferral of any nature, and this is why, from now on, the following question occurs to us: Was there ever "nature," since there was history, and thus an indefinite deferral of any nature? Was there ever a "prehistory," not only in the sense of a human prehistory, anterior to a history conceived and archived as such (the history contemporaneous with philosophy), but in the sense of a nonhuman prehistory, and even prior to life, a history of the world or of the Universe that had not already been always already historical in some way? This question leads to at least two others: that of knowing whether there can be some "posthistory," in whatever sense, and second, that of knowing whether it is possible, in a parallel and basically coessential or codetermined manner, of designating a pre- and/or a post philosophy . . .

Without claiming to confront these questions as such, here and now, we will agree perhaps there cannot not be in some fashion a "history of the world," if the world turns out not to have in itself its origin and its end, and that *even if, and especially if,* any "outside" of the world must be thought as *nothing,* and even if, and especially if, the meaning of the world is nothing other than the world itself in its originary and final relation with an infinite deferral of the origin and the end in that *nothing* of which it would be the expansion—that is to say, the growth or the creation (it is the same word) or even . . . the *history.*

There is thus a betrayal of the principle of history and of the world in the philosophical self-constitution and self-beginning. This betrayal reveals itself by the fact that philosophy must relinquish the task of thinking a history of the world if it is committed to a scheme of a proper emergence: for then it excludes thinking that the world outside of philosophy can be connected in any way to philosophical history. It is in a sense what, in the philosophical foundation, the division of *muthos* and *logos* signifies: this division [*partage*] is homologous, in the work of all the philosophers from Plato to Heidegger, with the scheme of self-constitution and its *aporias,* among which that of history is the most important.

But philosophy, at the same time (if it is the *same* time, if it is not an other time of another history that would remain to be written) reveals history. Indeed, the self-designation of philosophy as self-foundation, *self*-beginning, and *self*-completion, belongs to the same operation, which also consists in problematizing from the outset (and again at the *same* time) any structure and any process that is *auto*-constitutive and *auto*-referential. It is precisely by defining itself as an autonomous process and thus as history (philosophy *is* history and *makes* history as soon as Plato refers to its proper provenance in Anaxagoras,

Parmenides, and Socrates) that philosophy unveils the problematic order of an auto-constitution that must appropriate itself (that is to say, auto-constitute itself) through the mediation of its own temporal and genealogical difference along which the *auto-* alters itself primordially as much as it identifies itself. But, at the *same* time, it is outside of this history that the possibility of an auto-constitution was designated: in an order of *phusis* as the order of that which is for itself the gift and the immediate genesis of its own *nomos*, its own *technē*, and its own *logos*. But the logos, properly speaking, forms itself from that which it has to conquer, mediately, dia-*logically*, or *dia-lectically*, a *phusis* that is not given to it (or if one prefers a *phusis* that it gives itself only by immediately dividing from itself, *dia-lectically* and thus *historically*).

A remarkable chiasm occurs in which the "auto" and the "allo," the "by itself" and the "by the other," continuously exchange their places. This chiasm is the very emergence of philosophy, of the West, and of history. Instantaneously, and at the *same* time, two times are inaugurated: the *chronical* or *chronological* time of history and the *achronical* or *anachronical* time of an outside of history. But the first, the time of autochronic, in sum, is the time of difference or as difference, while the second as heterochronic (its time outside of time) will be the time (or the space) of given nondeferred identity. Philosophy constitutes this space-time as that of the *muthos*.

The following paradoxes result: at the same time the space-time of the *muthos* falls outside of history *and* becomes the first time or the prehistory of history, henceforth perfectly problematic since it is both inside and outside historicity. Now, this problem is nothing but the problem of the historicity of philosophy itself, and of the impossibility of thinking its own beginning: the proper beginning of the auto-beginning. In a parallel manner, by designating and instituting itself, philosophy designates an other—its other, its *proper* other—a regime of meaning and of truth: a regime of *allo*-constitution where the truth is given, but not to be conquered. In what philosophy baptizes as *muthos*, truth is given from an "outside" that is not a past and that is not the process of an (auto) production, which is immemorial and consequently always present, but is a presence, which escapes from the instantaneous instability of the philosophical present. Philosophy is the destabilization, the suspension, and the dissolution of the mythical present. This is why its obsessive fear becomes the present and the presence of time, or rather its absence, namely, *chronical* time. But in this way philosophy conceals its own presence, and its own coming to presence.

The withdrawal of the beginning belongs to the self-beginning. The beginning remains ungrounded.[1] The question opened by philosophy in its history and as history, the question opened by philosophical historicity as an essentially auto-constitutive dimension of philosophy, is the following: Is it or is it not possible to assume the nonfoundation of the beginning as the reason—thus as the ground—of the historical process itself? But this question is obviously nothing other than the following: Is it possible or not to assume the nonfoundation of the West as the reason for its own history? And since this history becomes the history of the world: is it possible or not to assume the nonfoundation of the history of the world? This means: Is it possible to *make* history, to *begin again* a history—or History itself—on the basis of its nonfoundation? Is it possible to assume both the absence of the auto-constitution (thus a relation to the prephilosophical other than the entirely problematic relation to the lost and desired exteriority of *phusis* and *muthos*) and the absence of auto-completion (thus the end of teleologies, theologies, and messianisms)?

2

Such a question is that of metaphysics and technology. If metaphysics, as such, itself essentially historical, accomplishes itself in the form of technology, and if technology must be understood as the planetary domination of the absence of beginning and end, or of the withdrawal of any initial or final *given*—of any *phusis* or of any *muthos*—how can one conceive of this process and thus conceive of history except according to the exhausted themes of progress and/or of decline, of the fortunate and/or unfortunate accident?

The completion of metaphysics—its *end* and its *plenitude*—happens in history insofar as it is precisely the accomplishment of the historical possibility itself, or the accomplishment of the "meaning of history" as it has been recognized at least since Nietzsche, but perhaps also, in a more complex manner, since Hegel himself, and in the way in which Husserl and Heidegger have attempted to grasp it as problem and as resource at the same time.

The historical possibility, properly speaking, as it was produced in its course by philosophy (or metaphysics: the possibility of a metaphysical history and a metaphysics of history) is the possibility that a process would complete the realization of a reason, of a ground, and of a rationality. It is thus the possibility that the historical process functions as a natural process. Metaphysical history is history thought as *physis*: as a "natural history," to use this old expression in which precisely "history" did not yet have the meaning of a process, but of a "collection." The truth of this history was that in the end, it denied itself as history by becoming nature (again).

In this elaboration, that which is exhausted is the *bringing to completion*. Whether the term is named presence, subject, Supreme Being, or total humanity, in each case the capacity of assumption and absorption of a *terminus ad quem* is exhausted. Very precisely, what is exhausted is nothing other than the exhausting itself in an end (*teleology*). Now, it is this exhaustion (accomplishment, maturation) that philosophy had constituted as a history after having remodeled according to Christian salvation, itself understood as a temporal process, the anamnesic movement of the Platonic u-topia or of the ec-topia. What is exhausted is thus the presence of a terminal present of history, a presence that would no longer be praesentia, being-ahead-of-itself, but only be equal to itself, in itself indifferent.

That the exhaustion is exhausted—that natural history breaks down and is *denatured*—is what is shown by the rupture that philosophy carries out by, in, or on itself: a historical rupture of its history, which Heidegger called the "end of philosophy" to indicate the depth and seriousness of that which in history thus happens to History, and by virtue of which a "history of being" or a "destinality" of its "sendings," perhaps even the end of the these sendings themselves, can only, at least, be *denatured*. But this *denaturation*[2] is what requires us to consider the extent to which, at what depth—properly without ground—history is not and cannot be auto-generating or *autotelic*, the extent to which, then, it cannot return to itself or in itself, or reabsorb itself in any "end of history." It requires us, on the contrary, to see finally, as if before us, the difference and the alteration of the *auto* that metaphysics, while producing it, first endeavored to cover or deny.

Consequently, if our expectation of the future is henceforth deprived of anticipation, of representation, and of concept, it must no less, like a Kantian judgment without concept, form a postulation of truth (and/or of universal) as a non-given truth: "denaturation" must itself be postulated as the "reason" of the process, of that history whose form is also that of an errancy. Non-given, neither as seed nor as completion—which also means, always, non-mythological—truth is first, as such, open and open to itself: it is the structure and the substance of an encounter with itself, awaiting and/or loyalty toward itself, toward the self that is not given. In this sense, truth empties itself of all presentable contents (whether one thinks of it in a sacral mode or in mode of positive knowledge). But this void is the void of the exhaustion of which I have spoken: truth is empty or rather emptied of any "content," of the plethora or the saturation of a completion, emptied of the plethora and therefore open in itself and on itself.

This means, above all, that it is open on the question of its own historicity. Truth—the truth of philosophy and of history—can do nothing else, henceforth, than open onto the abyss of its own beginning, or of its own absence of beginning, end and ground.

The historical gesture—that is, both the theoretical gesture with respect to "history," of its concept, *and* the practical, active gesture in our time, in order to appropriate this time, in order to *ereignen* another *story* [chronique] of the world—this gesture becomes then necessarily "deconstruction." To "deconstruct" means to disassemble what has built upon the beginnings in order to expose that which burrows beneath them. It is therefore the same thing to destabilize (not destroy) the structure of the philosophical (or metaphysical) tradition and to destabilize the historical auto-positioning of that tradition. What was built, from what beginnings and how these beginnings are determined as such—and still and perhaps above all, as I would like to show, what is the provenance of these beginnings? "Deconstruction" perhaps means nothing other, ultimately, than the following: it happens henceforth that philosophy cannot understand itself apart from the question of its proper historicity—and no longer only in the sense of its internal historicity, but also in the sense of its *external* provenance, but also in a way such that the external provenance and internal production are inextricably tied. (This is why it can only involve edges, extremities, ends, or limits of philosophy without, clearly, any accomplishment or completion. What else is, ultimately, at issue with Heidegger and with Derrida [who, in part despite Heidegger, opens again this dimension of deconstruction] if not the following: that philosophy cannot return to itself nor in itself as its *autology* requires, except by exceeding its autonomy and thus its own history in every respect?)

The beginnings of philosophy: the word must be written as plural, for it is not possible to name only one, but neither is it possible to name none. (To designate only one beginning would no doubt already submit to the metaphysical denial of alteration).[3] Philosophy certainly began as such and it stated that it began: no doubt it never stated *itself* without stating also that it begins and that it begins itself again. But the *subject*, which it wants to be, of this inauguration, undoes itself or destitutes itself, as we saw, in the very gesture of its inauguration. In this way, philosophy always institutes itself in a mixture of decision and indecision with respect to its own subject; and "deconstruction" in sum is congenital for it since it constructs itself on the understanding that it must be anterior to its edifice and even to its own plan.

This mixture of decision and indecision—or the decision of positing itself without a decision being reached about itself or about the immediately infinite mobilization of this decision—can be analyzed in a more precise manner. By beginning, philosophy prescribed to itself as its most proper law both an impossible *amanesis* (in the immemorial) of its own origin, and a blind perspective on the truth it awaits, to which it tends or seeks. On the one hand, philosophy presents itself as being without beginning or beginning by itself (who comes to free the prisoner from the cave?), and, on the other hand, truth absents itself in the obscurity or in the blinding light of what must come, insofar precisely as it

83

must come without ever arriving, like the last step, never reached or secured, which passes beyond the dialectical ascension, and which does not belong to the chronological time of succession and of accomplishment.

The double postulation of a return to the immemorial and an advance to what does not come designates what we call "metaphysics": a metaphysics that is said to be "ended," only in order to say that it exhausts that which claims to complete both its retrospection and prospection. Both must be incapable of ending: they must be the very incompletion conforming to the essence of philosophy, which turns out also to be indissociable from its history, its extended immobility (metaphysics) into the absenting of its origin and its end.

It follows from these premises that two claims must be set forth in the same moment: metaphysics is without beginning or end, and metaphysics begins and ends. It perhaps does not cease to begin and to end, the "without-beginning-or-end." It is in this sense that it is *finite*, in the structural and nondiachronic sense: it is finite in that it articulates a *non-given* of meaning or of some meaning (a "non-given" that constitutes, no doubt, the "void" of its truth: ontological finitude is what opens on the void—but it is being that is opened by this very opening, being insofar as it is not but opens itself in/as space-time). Structural finitude deconstructs historical endings [*finitions*] (for example, such figures as rationalism, empiricism, or criticism, and the figure of onto-theology, or even the figurative figure labeled as "onto-typology" by Lacoue-Labarthe). Similarly, with an unlimited scope, metaphysics itself always begins, has begun, and begins again, as *Abbau* of what is *gebaut* (and that always has the character of being a temple or a palace, of a residence and of a monument, thus also an empire or enterprise).

From the outset, or even ahead of itself, in a history underway before its history—between the twelfth and nineteenth century before our era—philosophy was the deconstruction of the edifices of a world that shook the mytho-religious world of given meaning, and of full and present truth. The unsettling of this world was the condition, perhaps already the beginning, of philosophy, of history, and of the "Western accident": and if one looks back toward what made this accident possible, one will presumably have to think even more so that it was hardly an "accident" in the ordinary sense (and perhaps hardly "Western" in the ordinary sense—the "West" having already preceded itself, and having been dispersed in the anterior history of the world, just as, today, it succeeds itself, disseminated in a becoming-world [*devenir-monde*]).

In the world where philosophy is born, a world within which a number of determinate technologies were developed (iron, writing, commercial accounting—to which we will return), tragedy begins as forming both the last testimony of cult and of sacrifice, and as the first attestation of a flight of meaning and of the abyss of truth: frankly, it is in this way that the terms or the concepts, or the questions of meaning and of truth are produced. The four conditions of philosophy identified by Badiou, which I mention here for their clarity, and whose names and notions are also produced in this moment—politics, science, art, and love—compose a four-part multiplication of this flight and of this opening. I will not dwell on the four dispositions of what one could call the inaugural *flight* [*échappée*] of the West: we see without difficulty how each is structured by this fleeing into *absens* (to borrow a word from Blanchot). Politics, science, love, and art are four structures of the impossible. At the same time, what the four have in common is another transversal dimension of the flight: namely, the incommensurability between the four "conditions" (an incommensurability that was unknown or, from the outset, reduced in a mythico-religious world). Philosophy is the common site of this incommensurability: it articulates flight or absence as the general regime of the incommensurable. What was later called metaphysics is thus produced as the articulation of that incommensurability: the very incommensurability of being in-itself, of being which *ex-ists* to itself, or that of the atelic and anarchic (this word in memory of Reiner Schürmann) principles and ends.

That metaphysics took place is not only a given fact (*de facto* in the history of a people, it takes place at a given moment, in the Mediterranean space and it is in this sense the *factum rationis empiricum* of philosophy—not without an Oriental *analogon*, which is given at the *same* time, constituted by Buddhism or Confucianism, an analogy that would need a long discussion) but still it is this very thing, this event that constitutes metaphysics. For it happened, it appeared as a flight, as a departure: namely, the flight of the Gods (a flight for which in the West monotheism is the first name, in itself already pregnant with the "death of God"—and one could add, what did Plato do if not weave together tragedy and monotheism just before Hellenistic Judaism, and then Christianity completed the work?). This flight is not simply an absenting, a leavetaking, or a suppression, neither is it an *Aufhebung* in the twofold Hegelian sense. It is above all a marking: a trace of an absence, a subtraction, to borrow from Badiou; a withdrawal, to borrow from Heidegger; an inscription, in the case of Derrida.

That is to say, the flight of the Gods traces or initiates an opening of an unprecedented meaning: in the same gesture, meaning is in flight as past and as to come—but *in the same stroke*, "meaning," is precisely and absolutely, the idea or the question of meaning (and of a truth that responds to it).[4]

If metaphysics begins as a science of principles and ends, this is because principles and ends are *crossed out* [*barrés*], if I can use the amphibology allowed by slang, crossed out and gone [*rayés et partis*] (slang also suggests *split* [*taillés*]), or else, in a more elaborate manner, divided from and in themselves, and thus "inscribed." It is only from the moment they are *crossed out* that they appear as such as "principles" and as "ends": subtracted from their very agency (from the foundation and realization of temples, empires, and lines of succession), open as questions of meaning.

3

Now, this subtraction—this subtraction/addition of meaning that constitutes philosophy from somewhere (in any case, it happens somewhere, in the contingency of a place and of a period, or of several places and several periods) or by some force (whose very occurrence is contingent: nothing determines the necessity of what takes place, although it does take place, potentially, at the scale of humanity and the world).

This force, in all respects, is that of *technology*. Behind what will become, in a very precise sense that we will need to analyze, *techno-logy*, there is a whole range of techniques, like that of iron followed by that of commerce (including both accounting and shipping), writing, and urban planning. With this moment in the history of technologies, there is a something like a threshold that is crossed. There is a movement that is contemporary to human beings—technology as human, quite simply *Homo faber*, producer and conceiver of *Homo sapiens*, technician of itself—a movement that from the outset proceeds by subtraction or by emptying out (from the loss of the *oestrus*, for example, until stone carving and wall painting) but which, until then, presents itself first as a mode of behavior and adaptation, as the management of subsistence conditions for an animal deficient in given conditions. This movement, which will always already have begun with "humans," and which consequently through humans, in humans, and before humans comes from "nature" itself, this very movement takes on another form: instead of ensuring subsistence, it creates new conditions for humans, or even produces a strange "surplus-subsistence" [*sursistance*] in nature or outside of it. The production of means of subsistence distinguishes already the Neolithic epoch: now—between the tenth and seventh century before our era on the arc of Asia Minor—one could say that a *production of ends* appears as such. But how could we not see this production of ends emerge—silently, secretly—from production that is itself not produced from nature or from the world, or from the animal or from man within it.[5] Consequently from what will we have to name history of the world?

With this becoming human, this movement appears to itself as its own principle and its own end. That is to say, properly without principle and without end since it proceeds from an initial detachment, which one can name

86

"human condition" and whose permanence involves an extreme instability and mutability of what has thus been detached (contingency forms thus the necessity of this "history"). And which is what we can call, feigning to believe that there would have been first a pure and stable "nature": *denaturation*. And one could then say that "humanity" is the indexical name of the indefinite and infinite term of the human denaturation.

It is in denaturation that something like the representation of a "nature" can be produced or of an autotelic order and thus nontechnological order that poses then at the same time the extreme difficulty of conceiving how denaturation arises from nature and in nature (how the deficient animal can be possible, the animal without set conditions). It is thus also there that comes forth, on the one hand, a specific technology of interrogation *peri phuseos* or *de natura rerum* at the same time as a thinking of the nonnatural origin of nature in the form of a "*creation ex nihilo.*" In these different ways, metaphysics constitutes from the outset the questioning of denaturation as such, in other words, of the escape from principles and ends, or of Being as nothing that is.

Such a questioning is made possible, indeed inevitable, as soon as a denaturing event took place: such is the event that we name "technology," with philosophy, which is itself the self-referential and self-reflective regime of that event. This event is part of a world, not only in the sense that the world, before any "history" has always already been its possibility (which therefore can be said to be neither necessary or contingent: any more or less that the world itself).

To say that there was something like a nature—*phusis* or *natura*, here one should not follow Heidegger's distinction between these names, as if he were marking the distance of a more "natural" nature, one that would not have harbored the possibility of human technology—is only possible if one contrasts this nature with a non-nature. In other words the very motif of "nature" is by itself "denaturing." The "physics" of the Presocratic Ionian is the technology of manipulation of the object "nature" that emerges when the mytho-religious order is disassembled: such a physics is a technology of crossed-out ends, and crossed-out principles.

The name of *metaphysics*, which appears then by accident, is in no way, in the end, accidental. It was already announced in the technological apparatus that produced "nature" as an object of both theoretical and practical manipulation, while seeing to it that "technology" clearly becomes a principle and an end for itself—as is the case in commerce, in writing *or* in the very production of principles and ends. This movement is necessarily a *becoming* since precisely what is at issue is what is not given and since technology in general is the know-how with respect to what is not already made: with technology, history is contrasted with nature. But it is just as necessary that this becoming not form a *meaning*, either progressive or regressive. The obsession with meaning, which nonetheless will have determined an entire section of metaphysics, is only the recurrent effect of a mytho-religious "physics" seeking to reconquer itself in spite of metaphysics or through it. This is why metaphysics is continually in the radical ambivalence of an opening and of a closure or in the difficult topology that allows a closure by an opening and an opening by a closure.

If there is a "meaning" of the world according to technology, it can only be measured by an incommensurable standard of the non-necessity and of the nonnaturality of the world (that is to say, of the totality of possible *signifyingness*), which also implies its nonhistoricity in the metaphysical and theo-teleo-logical sense of the word *history*. Such a meaning, such an *absence* and such an "*absentheism*" are quite precisely those of the technological event itself.

There is thus a precondition that makes the logical and philosophical conditions of the Western accident possible. This precondition is indissociably historical, technological, and transcendental—which also means necessary as the reason of philosophy as metaphysics, and nevertheless contingent because there is no sufficient reason of this reason—if not the general and congenital (connatural) denaturation of nature that always already harbors, without necessity and without contingency, just as the universe itself is neither necessary nor contingent, the possibility of technological man.

(Rousseau, it seems, is the foremost thinker—therefore also the most problematic—of this infinitely twisted denaturing inscription in nature itself, which is also the inscription of the flight of the gods.) Politics, science, art, and love (a fourfold that, upon reflection, is very Rousseauian) each respond, with mutual incommensurability, to the technological condition in its state of metaphysical autonomization. Each is structured by the unassignable character of its own principle and end, each is a technology or a technological configuration, or rather each opens onto an indefinite chain of technological transformations. This fourfold is as conditioned as conditioning with respect to philosophy.

(One could also articulate each of the four by showing that each serves as an end for the other three, in a way that the structure remains always open and cannot be totalized and that, in addition, each "end" is incommensurable with the others while forming simultaneously the *telos* and the limits of the others.)

But this is also, or first, why philosophy as such *begins*: it begins as a *technology* of meaning and/or of truth. In this sense, it is not at all a prolongation of the mytho-religious world, nor its overcoming by progress, nor its *Aufhebung*, nor its decline or its loss: it is the technological reinscription of "nature" and of the "gods." When meaning is denatured—or demythified—truth emerges as such: it is a matter of constructing meaning (the principle and end of Being as such) or else punctuating *absence* [absens] and, finally, with the two always implicated in any metaphysical construction and deconstruction worthy of the name. It is not a surprise that sophistry, at a given moment, becomes the correlation and counterpoint of a technological complex (once again commerce, law, urban planning, city—in Asia Minor during the time of the pre-Socratics). It is not only a technology of *logos*, which is invented and organized along with other technologies. With the very concept of *logos*, reaching from the order of discourse to that of verifying autonomy, it is a technology that manages production, no longer of subsistence, nor even of a surplus subsistence, but of meaning itself. It is in this sense that I therefore name metaphysics a *techno-logy*: the flight into a verifying autonomy of technology, or of "denaturation." But this autonomy repeats in an infinite abyss, all of the constitutive aporias of the *auto-* in general.

One should thus wonder whether this explains why philosophy with Socrates was presented straightaway as a dialogue with technologies or their meta-technological interpellation: beginning with Sophistry, and modeling itself on mathematics, the arts of the cobbler, carpenter, or in general. Similarly one will recall that Aristotle considered that philosophy could only happen beyond the satisfaction of the necessity of subsistence:[6] as if it itself was the opening of another genre of satisfaction, but in a continuity or in an analogy of the technological posture. (We can also consider the *wonder* that Aristotle designates in the same passage [and after Plato] as the beginning of philosophy designates nothing other than the technology proper to a non-knowing: not ignorance waiting for a teacher, nor inexperience in the process of being initiated—which are both modalities of the mytho-religious world—but the knowledge that articulates itself, first, on its own abyss.)

One could also consider—and I cannot dwell on it as would be necessary—the possibility, indeed the necessity of determining the history of technologies up to our time without giving it another meaning in its fundamental contingency than the indefinite relation of technology to itself and to the escape of its denaturation. One would have to examine, in this respect, the succession of technologies of the immediate supplementation of the human body (tools, arms, clothing), of the production of subsistence (agriculture, animal husbandry), of exchange (money, writing), then, with another turn, of meaning and truth (sophistical, philosophical), of wealth as such, of production itself (capital, labor), of society (democracy) and finally, of nature itself, or of its complete denaturation, whether by mutation or by total destruction (biological, ecological, ethological engineering) . But what would then give the tone and the direction of this series, its principle and its end, nonetheless without principle or end, would be the "architechnology," the pro-duction of the pro-ducer, or the ex-position of the exposed, the "nature" of man as the denaturation in him of the whole of "nature," what we call today the "symbolic," in other words the opening of an empty space where the infinite "creation" of the world is (re)played—unless the possibility arises that the symbolic is barred there and disappears there and with it humanity itself.

The event of technology—that is to say, for us, for a long time, history and metaphysics as history—would thus have a meaning in a sense that would be neither directional nor significant: but in the sense that we say that "someone has business sense," for example, or "a musical sense," or in general when one "has a sense" of this or that technology, in that sense, then, this would be the sense of principles and ends (of being as such or of existence) there, where, quite precisely neither end, nor principles, nor being are given or available, and where existence exposes itself, lacking sense, making this lack its very truth. Metaphysics is the name of this sense: the *savoir-faire* of denaturation, or of the infinitization of ends. This implies above all not a knowledge, but an *ethos*: *logos* itself as *ethos*, that is to say, the technology or the art of *standing in and abiding* in the escape of the *absence*. The art of standing, or what permits in general having or maintaining a standing in, including, and especially, where there is no longer any support or firm basis for whatever stance there is.

IV

Complements

1

A Note on the Term: *Biopolitics*

We have heard quite a bit in recent years about the term *biopolitics*. This word was created by Foucault. It has been used by several theoreticians in various senses. The variety of these senses and a certain general indetermination of the term require a clarification.

In particular, the use of similar terms such as "bioethics" furthers the confusion since "bioethics" is concerned with the moral decisions made when confronted by the new possibilities of biological technology (or of "biotechnology") and does not claim to designate an ethics generally restricted to the *bios*.[1] "Biopolitics," on the contrary, seeks to indicate the order of a politics generally determined by life and devoted to its maintenance and control. What is meant by biopolitics, in principle, is not "a politics about life or living" but, rather, "life determining politics," or else "the sphere of politics coextensive with the sphere of life."[2]

For Foucault, in a more narrow way, the word designated the fact that, from the eighteenth century on, the control of the conditions of human life[3] became an expressly political affair (health, nutrition, demographics, exposure to natural and technological dangers, etc.). Until that time, power had little interest in this and had other objects for its exercise: first and foremost, territory. I have nothing to add to this historical thesis, which is certainly important, except that it seems to me that it would require a more precise examination of what the biopolitical preoccupations were before the modern era (there was a politics of wheat in Rome and a politics of birth in Athens, for example).

Foucault considered that totalitarian politics—Nazi first, socialist as well— were biopolitics because they were devoted, rather than to the domination of their adversaries, to the mastery of a population, of a "race," or of a "people" defined according to norms of health, or productive vitality, etc. (Foucault ranks everything under a very general category of "racism.") Here I will not enter into the precise examination of these theses. I believe it necessary, however, to ask if "life" truly constitutes the object (real or imaginary, is not the issue now) of these powers, or if it is not rather a destinal figure ("race" or "the human worker") that comes to substitute for the classical figures of sovereignty. The reduction of these figures to "life" is not sufficient to ground their political and affective power.

According to the extension recently given to the concept, or rather according to that which is in reality a changing of the concept under the same word, it seems one must understand the following: politics (still assigned to the State) progressively takes for its object the controlled management of natural life.

However, it is clear that so-called "natural life," from its production to its conservation, its needs, and its representations, whether human, animal, vegetal, or viral, is henceforth inseparable from a set of conditions that are referred to as "technological," and which constitute what must rather be named *ecotechnology* where any kind of "nature" develops for us (and by us). That life is precisely the life that is no longer simply "life" if one understands it as auto-maintaining and auto-affecting. What is revealed, rather, with ecotechnology, is the infinitely problematic character of any "auto" in general. It is in this context that a "biopolitics" is possible, since it is defined by a technological management of life. This supposes that existence thus managed is no longer, tendentiously, an existence that engages anything else than its reproduction and its maintenance through finalities that remain the secrets of power, unless they are simply blind or purposeless finalities of the eco-technological totality in motion.

Thus *bios*—or life as a "form of life," as the engagement of a meaning or of a "being"—merges with *zōē*, bare life, although such life has, in fact, already become *technē*.

Politics is thus implicitly nothing other than the auto-management of ecotechnology, the only form of possible "auto"-nomy that precisely no longer has recourse to any heretofore possible forms of a politics: neither the self-founding "sovereignty,"[4] since it is no longer a matter of founding, nor the "discussion concerning the justice" of an Aristotelian *polis*, since there is no longer a *polis*, nor even the contestation or the *differend*, since living and power go in the same direction according to an asymptomatic consensus and devoid of finality, or of truth.

The term *biopolitics* in fact designates neither life (as the form of life) nor politics (as a form of coexistence). And we can certainly admit that in fact we are no longer in a position to use either of these terms in any of their ordinary senses. Both are, rather, henceforth subject to what carries them together into ecotechnology.

But then the danger of the word is revealed in that it seems to authorize two forms of interpretations, both of which surreptitiously maintain an unusual sense of the term. One can attempt to think that this life, reduced to an absence of form other than its management motivated by an economic and social power that only seeks its maintenance, finds itself dialectically delivered to an absence of ends through which it would find itself as though in its nascent state, exposed to the absence of the meaning of its bare contingency, such that it would be therefore capable of reclaiming as its own invention: an indefinite birth, sliding by its very errancy and by its absence of justification outside of the domination that manipulates it. The form of life would be the furtive play of an elegant withdrawal from the grinding machine. One can think on the contrary that the control thus revealed of a technological production of life places life in the state of producing itself as a whole, and of reappropriating the exteriority of domination in a common auto-production or auto-creation whose vitality reabsorbs and accomplishes, in itself, any politics.

In one way or another, by an emphasis upon life itself or politics reappropriated in common, what is put into play again is the twofold dialectical postulation by which, on the one hand, an extreme figure (previously known as the proletariat) is revealed—the bareness of which establishes its truth-character—while, on the other hand, the power reappropriated by the living community effectuates the negation of political separation. This figuration and this negation have haunted the Western consciousness ever since the invention of democracy put an end to politics founded on figures of identification. But it is clearly insufficient to seek a new figure (whether figureless, anonymous, and stripped of identity), or to render dialectical the negation of the identificatory pole. These two motifs, opposed or conjoined, can give momentum, perhaps, to necessary struggles—and there are numerous. But they cannot address the problem opened by democracy, that is to say, a problem posed by ecotechnology that demands, or that produces, the absence of separable figure and the absence of identifiable end: because until this point it was between figures and ends, between phenomenalization of a teleology and a teleology of a phenomenalization, that any part of life and/or of politics, of meaning of life, or of form of politics, has operated.

It is not a question here of developing this clarification further. At least it should serve to show that what *forms a world* today is exactly the conjunction of an unlimited process of an eco-technological enframing *and* of a vanishing of the possibilities of forms of life and/or of common ground. The "world" in these conditions, or "world-forming," is only the precise form of this problem.[5]

2

Ex Nihilo Summum (Of Sovereignty)

Sovereignty designates, first, the summit.[6] For the pleasure of language, let us refer to *ès souvereinités des monts*, a twelfth-century translation of *in summus montium* (in the Latin Vulgate bible, cited by La Curne).[7] The summit towers over and dominates. (*Summus, supremus, superanus* are—in sum—linguistic cousins.) One has said "a large tower that is master and sovereign of the door of the castle" (Ibid.). The fate of the word in language pertains to the attribution of domination to the summit and, consequently, to the analogical parallel between height and power (to which one can add the implication of value or excellence). This parallel is itself doubled in the origin of the *summa*, which pertains to the fact that the sum of the addition was inscribed on the *summa linea*, since the Romans calculated from the base to the height.

It follows as well from this history that sovereignty is not first of all the quality of being at the summit but the summit itself (a term that has a botanical sense as well as academic), the summit, the sovereign: it does not have the sense of an attribute but that of the substance of a subject whose being consists in height.

The highest dominates properly only according to the military sense indicated by the example of the "large tower": from on high it is easier to survey and strike what is below. Summits have always been places of fortresses and citadels. But then warlike domination immediately involves elevation and altitude raised to the sky, standing out against the sky, and penetrating into it. The sovereign communicates with the element detached from the earth, freed from gravity. In the same way the *chief* or the head (the captain, the capital or capitol) rises above the ground by virtue of the erect stance of the body of the biped whose straight stance (haughty carriage) casts the gaze into the distance, separates the hands from the feet, distances the sense of smell from the soil and from its genitals. But the sovereign is more than a chief: the chief extends and completes a body; the sovereign rises above the body.

The sovereign is at the height because the height separates the top from the bottom and frees the former from the humility of the latter: from the humus, from the back bent from working the earth, from laying down in sleep, from malady or death, and from *extended things* in general. Extension holds everything at the same level, but the thing that is not extended, what looms over extensions and inspects it, is the *thinking thing* and the subject of the general government of things. In the place of a sensibility of the near, through touch, smell and taste, it makes the organs of distance, sight and hearing, prevail. The sovereign is not content to react to what surrounds and neighbors it; it gathers information about messages and dispositions from distant realities with the aim of being able to impose its law on them. (The emblems of the sovereign are the eagle and the sun.)

The sovereign is elevated because height separates. The separation ensures the distinction and the distinction ensures the differentiation of levels necessary to establish a hierarchy that is less a sacred commandment than the sacred character of a commandment, or of government as such: its separate, discrete, secret, and withdrawn nature. Its withdrawal gathers it in itself by removing it from the dependency of things pressed against each other, entangled in the action and reactions of the others. The sovereign is separated from this dependence and this endless exchange of means and ends. It is itself neither a means nor an end. It is of another order, of an order that indexes any horizontality, its thickness and its connections, on a perpendicular verticality. The sovereign does not only tower over: it is transversal.

As summit (*summum, supremus*), the sovereign is not only elevated: it is the highest. Its name is a *superlative*: literally what raises itself above from below, and what is no longer comparable or relative. It is no longer in relation, it is *absolutum*.

The sovereign is the highest, it is the extremity of elevation: it is the most high. The Most High is the one whose height is no longer relative, and even not relative to lesser heights. It is Height itself, all height and nothing but height (grammatically, it is in fact what we call an absolute superlative). The Most High does not allow measurement. It escapes observation while at the same time it is inaccessible to scaling. It does not exactly pertain to the opposition between the top and the bottom but rather to the difference between the height and what has neither height nor depth (*altus* has both senses). The Most High is the Inequivalent itself. It is not equivalent to any kind of equivalence or inequivalence. It is, to the contrary, on its basis alone that something like the register of equivalence or inequivalence can be posited.

The Most High is the one or that toward which the head itself cannot turn without toppling immediately off the axis that attaches it to the body. It ceases then to be the head. Either it loses itself in the height or it falls back into the equivalence of the body with itself.

The Most High can only produce one thing: vertigo. The vertigo is that which takes hold at the summit. *Vertex* is another name for the summit. It is the point where the *vertical* is at its peak: it returns there (*vertere*) on itself, no longer having room to go higher since it is the highest possible elevation. Vertigo is the affect of the summit. It is the apprehension of the incommensurability between the horizontal and the vertical, between the base and the summit. It is the vertigo of the absolute insofar as it is without any relations: in the absence of the slightest relation it can only turn on itself. But it is in this sense that the sovereign must determine any establishment of relations or their regulations.

The sovereign has had a certain twin in language and in thought: the suzerain. The two terms have at times shared or exchanged their significations. They also have the same root in the *sus*, the *dessus*, and the *au-dessus*. They are two forms of the *superior*. However, in the end, the sovereign is incommensurable with the suzerain. This is precisely the meaning of the transition from feudalism to the modern political age.

The suzerain occupies a certain height within an ordered system. The suzerain has the vassal (originally the servant) beneath it. Vassal and suzerain are bound to each other by a reciprocal oath of allegiance and assistance. The oath pledges fidelity, that is to say, loyalty. The feudal order—which involves the regime of the *fief*—rests on the loyalty pledged between vassals and suzerains. This loyalty is exercised in both directions, and within the fief, which is the domain over which the lordship rules, which, at first, is the authority of the elder (*senior*).

The elder is not the highest: the succession of ages depends on nature, it does not define—not exactly or entirely—a difference in the same way that height does. The elder is always behind one older still, even if the dead father. The right is thus an ancestral one: it is not conferred according to the absoluteness of height in itself. This is why there are several heights of lordship, and the *sire* (the other name for lord) can be duke or marquis, simple knight or baron. Here, the bond, the manifold of bonds that founds the *fiefs* and the vassalages, takes precedence over power; it gives it its *raison d'être*. In a certain manner, power is here bound from the outset.

In the case of sovereignty, on the contrary, it is power that founds and forms the bond. The bond is not one of loyalty but authority, in the precise sense that the sovereign is the author of the law, whereas loyalty supposes a law that precedes it.

The feudal order is itself subordinated to an authority that surpasses any suzerain: that of the only lord that merits the title in an absolute sense, Our Lord, the All-Mighty, the creator and redeemer of the world. No doubt, historically, the feudal order was nevertheless the source of the conditions of a duality of powers—temporal and spiritual—which opens the way to an autonomy of the first. But the feudal order only becomes properly autonomous with the principle (this is indeed the right term: it is the province of the Prince) of sovereignty. The sovereign is not a suzerain among others; it is freed from any bond. Therefore, it no longer has vassals, only subjects.

(On this account the entire world will become subject and the lowest vassals will no longer have servants beneath them, servants attached to the glebe.

There will no longer be an eminent property of the glebe, but on the contrary the subjects will all become proprietors. With respect to the proprietor in the modern sense, the suzerain disappears without becoming sovereign. The suzerain has authority, but it is not due to its property. It does not have to give it a law but has only to enjoy it, or if this word is too noble, to profit from it.)

The subject of the sovereign can be understood in two ways: as the one who is subjected to the authority of the sovereign, or as the one who creates and authorizes this authority. This amphibology leads in a continuous manner from monarchy to democracy. The sovereign people possess nothing less and nothing more than the absolute monarch: namely, the very exercise of sovereignty.

This exercise is nothing other than the establishment of the State and of its law, or of the law that makes a State. It supposes that nothing either precedes it or supercedes it, that no authority or instituting force has been exercised before it. Sovereignty is the end of any political theology: if it borrows the figure of divine law it does so precisely to model this figure on the features of the sovereign. These features are defined by the following amphibology: it is the subject of the exercise to which it is subjected.

Where divine authority operated between creator and creature—that is to say, through an absolute difference in nature, but where the creature came from the act of the creator—there, the difference disappears in favor of an exceptional identity, which is precisely that of the sovereign. Whatever its concrete determination may be (republic of a prince, of a council, or a people), sovereignty must be identical to itself in its institution and its exercise. It has no outside to precede, found, or duplicate.

The sovereign is a relation to itself (to itself as to the law), and it is only that (while the creator is essentially only a relation to the other, and the bond of loyalty also depends on this relation). A twofold consequence follows from this:

- The first concerns the so called motif of "secularization": without wishing to enter into the immense debate around this concept, I suggest simply here that modern sovereignty (sovereignty as a modern concept, the one that is attributed expressly to Jean Bodin[8] and also anticipated in the work of Machiavelli) is not the secularization of a divine sovereignty, precisely because divine sovereignty contains, by definition, the supreme reason and power that modern sovereignty is assigned with giving;
- The second consequence consists in referring to the sovereign the constitutive problematic of the relation to self or of auto position in general: the self of a relation to self cannot be given prior to this relation itself, since it is the

relation that makes the self (*self* means relation *to self* and there is no case in which there is a subject of *self*). The sovereign does not find a sovereignty that is given: it must constitute it and thus constitute itself as sovereign.

Each of these implications contain, in turn, several others, and in particular:

- From the first, it is necessary to conclude that God, or the divine, in general, can in no way be "secularized," since "secularity" designates the order external to divinity, which can only be understood in a regime of distinction (either mortal/immortal, or century/eternity, or world/kingdom of God); it means either that politics can never absorb religion if religion has a proper consistency or that there is no autonomous religion and that it is always the instrument of a politics that through it gives itself the ultimate agency of authority and of legitimacy (perhaps that must yet be stated otherwise, by distinguishing religion as always political in one way or another, and the relation to the divine that should be named otherwise, a point that I leave open here).
- From what precedes, one will conclude also that the possibility of the distinctions thus presented pertains to the Western-monotheistic articulation of the "divine": in what is called "polytheism" there is no separation of politics and religion (in a sense one could say there is neither one nor the other); for monotheism, on the contrary, there is a tension between the separation of the two and the effacement of the one by the other.
- From the second implication, one will conclude that sovereignty can only be defined as an institution (in the active and transitive sense of the term, and here precisely as an institution of self)—an infinite institution that nevertheless includes within it the imperious necessity of the finite moment of its institution (this time in the conjunctive senses of the instituting and the instituted): there is thus an intimate contradiction of sovereignty and, through it, of modern politics, (that is, atheological), which is perhaps also, as I just suggested, politics pure and simple.

The sovereignty of the people designates very clearly, in Rousseau's work, the most radical state of the sovereign contradiction: in distinction from the monarch who could hide behind a divine reference, however formal it may be, as sovereign the people must be understood as the subject or the body that forms itself: such is the object of the contract that becomes, in Rousseau, in addition to a pact of security, the very institution of the contractors and their body, in other words, humanity itself as it is stated in *The Social Contract*.[9] The sovereign people are a people who constitute themselves as subjects in all senses of the word: namely, as the self-relation of each in the relations of all to the others and as the subjection of all to this relation. But since the relation to self is infinite, the people is also infinitely lacking to, or in excess of itself.

In this sense, the modern political question could be reduced to the question of sovereignty: Doesn't it define the political impasse *par excellence* as the impasse of subjectivity? And, if that is the case, can we either conceive of a nonsubjective sovereignty or conceive of a nonsovereign politics? Or rather, must we think of the two things together?

Sovereignty itself, as a summit, poses the problem of the nature of the summit. What is its relation to the base and what results from it for its proper constitution? Does the summit rest on the base, does it lean on it, or does it detach from it and accede to another ontological sphere?

Is the summit the region, tangential to the sky, where elevation takes place, reverses the ascent into a descent and, thus returning upon itself, attaches its height to the soil, giving it thus both its equilibrium and its dimension? Or is it the point where the elevation becomes absolute, cutting itself from the soil and from the base and indicating a completely different agency that relates less to what it overhangs than to the fact that nothing hangs over it?

In the first hypothesis, the summit subsumes and assumes the base that, after all, is *its* base, the foundation and the seat of its own being. But in this sense, the highest is never the Most High, never the absolute height. It is always situated at a relative altitude, and, finally, no doubt it is always, at bottom, *primus inter partes*. This also implies that this summit is in an essential relation with a bottom, which is also a ground, a seat, a place, and an assurance that is also a resource and a *capital* of authority, of legitimacy, and of the power of execution.

And since I have spoken of capital: In this acceptation, is the summit the same as capital? Or more exactly, does capital proceed from that structure according to which the summit accumulates and enables the resources of the base, as well as its productions from the place where they do not simply reproduce the base itself? To what extent is capital—which I understand clearly here in the Marxist sense—linked to sovereignty? To what extent is the nontheological autonomy of the State substantially linked to the accumulation—also nontheological—of wealth, that is to say, of the riches that no longer shine for a sacred glory but for itself and for its own production? With capital, in any case, it is clear that the summit accomplishes an accumulation of a mass, a sum, and that this mass must not cease to grow: the capital is sovereign in the sense that it only serves itself. The word *capital* defines wealth as sovereign: it is distinguished from the wealth that serves the needs of necessity, and from the wealth that serves no purpose except to concentrate (and that dispenses and that disperses) a hierophantic *éclat*. Here we find the reason for the coupling of the sovereign modern state and capital: the auto finality, which also presents itself as a finality without end, or in the auto princedom that gives itself its own investiture.

In the second hypothesis, sovereignty is essentially different from mastery, according to the way of thinking that was, to the point of paroxysm, that of Bataille. Mastery may very well only serve itself but it is still a service: it submits to its project, or to the project that it is. The master is himself the project of subjecting the slave to himself, and, through the slave, of assuring a means of existence, which forms the order to which the slave has submitted from the outset. The master is submitted to this submission, which is, in the last account, submission to means geared to an end whose final dignity remains obscure: Why must existence maintain itself (as if it belonged to these things whose being seems constituted by an inert persistence)?

Under these conditions the sovereign is the one who detached itself from mastery and its fundamental servility. It is not that the sovereign renounces mastery, at least not as a good that it would abandon for a superior good. The sovereign does not weigh or calculate mastery according to some scale of values. It stands exclusively and straightaway at the height of absolute value.

This height is thus altitude in itself, elevation that has ascended to the summit without the ascension representing any process of accumulation or conquest, any progression toward an end. In truth, it cannot even be a question of ascending to the summit. It is a detached summit, without any contact with the outside of the whole structure built upon the base: and since this outside is nothing, and there can be no question of access, or an access that can be immediately experienced as a penetration into nothing, sovereignty turns out strictly to be that *nothing* itself. (As we know, Bataille was given to write, "sovereignty is NOTHING," where the capital letters are meant to raise an infinite irony in the face of any effort to capitalize the absolute sovereign.)

Not being anything [*rien*] or, even more precisely, being nothing, sovereignty is nonetheless some thing: it is that very particular thing that *nothing* [rien] is. Not "the nothing," as if it was an entity, and specifically, the entity of a negation of being. That is what is called, "nothingness" ["*le néant*"]. Nothingness is not nothing [rien]: it is that which being turns into as soon as it is posited for itself and as unilateral. Whether one considers, with Hegel, that being pure and simple is pure abstraction, or one thinks with Heidegger that being, or *to be*, cannot be something that is an entity, one must resolve to think of being as its own effacement that negates it and, while negating it, allows for the spacing of the concrete. There is no ontology without the dialectic or the paradox of a meontology.

On the other hand, *nothing* [rien] is the thing itself, *res*: the first sense of "nothing" is "some thing"(for example, we still say today: "It is not possible to think nothing about something we know nothing about," where we clearly hear "something"). If *nothing* has slid, through the negation "no . . . thing" ["*ne . . . rien*"] to a privative sense, it is by keeping the sense of "the thing": "one must think nothing" signifies "one must think no thing," thus, "not a thing, not a single thing." *Nothing* is the thing tending toward its pure and simple being of a thing, consequently also toward the most common being of *something* and thus toward the vanishing, momentary quality of the smallest amount of being-ness [*étantité*].

That which is nothing is what subsists this side of or beyond subsistence, of substance and of subject. It is what realizes or reifies existence right where it is detached from its own position: right where it exceeds the stance, the station, and the stability of beings. This point is its contact with the being that permeates it: it is the point of cancellation of the *ontological* difference. But this difference is cancelled only through being infinitely sharpened. It is thus the point where existence exists as the engaging of its very being. Heidegger names it *Dasein*: being the "there," being that "there," which is the very point where the entity itself opens being.

The sovereign is the existent who depends upon nothing—no finality, no order of production or subjection, whether it concerns the agent or the patient or the cause or the effect. Dependent upon nothing, it is entirely delivered over to itself, insofar as precisely, the "itself" neither precedes nor founds it but is the *nothing*, the very thing from which it is suspended.

Nothing as a summit, *acme*, or height of existence: separated from the existent itself.

Sovereignty essentially eludes the sovereign.

If sovereignty did not elude it, the sovereign would in no way [*en rien*] be sovereign.

The same condition that ensures that sovereignty receive its concept also deprives it of its power: that is, the absence of superior or foundational authority. For the sovereign authority must be essentially occupied with founding itself or with overcoming itself in order to legislate prior to or in excess of any law. In a rigorous sense, the sovereign foundation is infinite, or rather, sovereignty is never founded. It would, rather, be defined by the absence of foundation or presupposition: neither in Athens nor in Rome was there a pure absence of presupposition prior to the law. Something of the divine or of destiny remains.

On that basis, if the sovereign exercises its power, it is entirely on the condition of the "state of exception" where laws are suspended. The fundamental illegitimacy that is in this case the condition of legitimacy must legitimize itself. That can be understood in terms of what Carl Schmitt calls "political theology," given that this theology, nevertheless, is in no way theological, or it only retains from theology an atheological idea of all-powerfulness. One encounters again the debate on secularization, where we could say that Schmitt conserves the attributes of God without its person, while Blumenberg proposes to think that without the person the attributes also change their change.

What then is the all-powerfulness of the people? This is the question. And perhaps it is absolutely necessary for democracy to be able to envisage this question while maintaining the principle of the *nothing* of sovereignty. Being nothing, or being founded on nothing, does not mean being powerless [ne *rien pouvoir*]: it means to found and measure power by that *nothing* which is *the very thing* of *the reality* of the people: its nature as nonfoundational, nontranscendent (at least in the usual sense), nonsacred, nonnatural etc. *Res publica, summa res—nihil.*

If sovereignty is not a substance that is given, it is because it is the *reality* that the people must give themselves, insofar as it is not, itself, a substance or a given subject. A people are always their own invention. But it can also invent itself by giving itself a sovereign and by giving itself *to* a sovereign or even by giving the sovereignty to itself. In each case the people determine themselves differently and determine the very sense of the word *people* differently: assembled people, subjected people, insurgent people—or rather: people as a body, people as a group, people in secession. Constituting sovereignty, alienating sovereignty, revolutionary sovereignty. It is always a matter of the combinatory, of the intersection or the disjunction of these agencies: and, consequently, of what remains between them as the empty space of sovereignty "itself."

As the highest, the absolutely high, the sovereign detaches itself from the bottom. There is no longer a relation to the bottom. The sovereign does not even look from top to bottom. It does not behoove it to descend nor condescend. The sovereign only has a relation with what is not the bottom as the correlate of the top, following the measure of a scale, but rather the depth, the correlate of the elevated according to the boundlessness [*démesure*] of the absolute: the depth and the altitude are equally detached (ab-solute).

The sovereign and the founder are correlates and conjoined as two absolutes or two sides or moments of the same absolute. The one who founds is sovereign (this is the dynastic, imperial, familial, hierarchical, and hierophantic aspect)—the line of the furrow by which Romulus consecrates the soil—and the one who is sovereign founds (this is the princely, singular, decisive aspect that seizes opportunities—the strike of the sword brought by Romulus to Remus).

The ambiguity of sovereign violence is between these two blades, of the plow or of the sword, or in the fact that the same blade can serve both purposes. But it lies equally in the fact that the foundation is without ground, and that the furrow where one lays the first stone is also a gaping gash.

Today, however, we are not in this ambiguity: we are not able to grasp a founding violence (or what could be the prolongation of it: a war that one could call "just"—whether it be a foreign war—between established sovereignties—or a civil war—in order to retake or refound a sovereignty). Violence has become unilateral. It appears then, and sovereignty with it, as pure violence, straightaway and definitively deprived of legitimacy, openly installing its illegitimacy in the guise of power. That this violence is increasingly realized as a violence of capital means that the *sum* is installed in the place of the *summit*, and hence the infinity of the accumulation in the place of the absolute in act. The coupling of the sovereign state and capital enters into dehiscence. Self-foundation and self-accumulation become heteronomous. Capital no longer has a need of the State (or in a limited way), and the State no longer knows on what to found itself or what it founds.

In a parallel way, capital no longer needs borders—at least many of them, and that which replaces the borders is of the order of a delimitation of "zones," which are of a different order. With the border, with the territory and with the nation-state, local constraints, subjections forbidding access to the production of humanity by itself and subservience to particular sovereignties disappear. But the marks of sovereign determination are also effaced: a circumscription that permits the inscription of a summit. There is no world summit: or would it be necessary, rather, to conceive of the world itself, not according to a renewed sovereignty but in place of any sovereignty?

Posed in Marxian terms, the question is of knowing if, how, and when the process of capital makes necessary and possible, not the restoration of state-based sovereignty, but the reclamation of sovereignty at its roots, which is *nothing* and in this *nothing* the thing itself, which is precisely not a root but the summit, the inverted radicality of the uncompromising, inconsistent, and absolutely resistant summit: the summit as *ex nihilo*, whence a world can emerge—or its contrary.

Or perhaps it is a question—in other terms or by slightly shifting the problem—of separating politics from sovereignty.

That is to say that it would be a question then of assuming that "politics" no longer designates the assumption of a subject or in a subject (whether individual or collective, whether conceived as a natural organic unity, or as a spiritual entity, as an Idea, or as a Destiny), but designates the order of the subjectless regulation of the relation between subjects: as individual as collective or communitarian subjects, groups of different kinds, families of different sorts, interest groups, whether labor or leisure, local or moral affinities, etc. The main axiom here would be that these groupings are not subsumable under a sole common being of superior rank.

The political order would define its regulation by an equality and by a justice that would not postulate an assumption of a subject. In that sense politics would be subjectless: not that it does not require agents, but it would not claim to form by itself a place of identity or a return to the self. It would, on the contrary, define a space without return to the identical.

One needs to consider the following:

1. The invention of sovereignty has decidedly not been the secularized transcription of a political theology but the creation of an atheological assumption (echoing, to be sure, something of the Greek *polis* and of the Roman Republic, but without the resource of a religion of the polis and without slavery—and in a generally atheistic and capitalistic context): this assumption postulated both, without knowing it, the institution of the State (self-stability) *and* the dissolution of that State (or apparatus) in a community—a contradictory postulation whose dissolution we are dealing with;

2. The current situation is that of having to reinvent politics otherwise, by reconsidering it on the basis of its double withdrawal, in the management of "civil society" (itself issued from a dehiscence of the *civitas*) and/or in the assumption of a common being (destinal and ontological sense of "politics").

Neither of these withdrawals guarantees a politics: but they produce, on the one hand, *management*[19] that manages nothing, and on the other hand, the paranoia of identity, which demolishes all identities. It follows that the twofold withdrawal traces the contours of what remains to be: an agency that regulates the organization of the common without the assumption of a common substance or subjectivity.

The difficulty is of conceiving of politics without a subject: not without authority or decision-making power—but without a self that reaps, in the end, the benefits of its action. The difficulty is as simple as it is daunting: namely, that power, without which it is pointless to speak of politics, is only exercised against its will. This is the problem of equality in which political modernity consists— and sovereignty itself, as soon as it defines a summit that is not measured by any given height. Liberty and fraternity, together, could represent this absence of given height (of foundation, of father). The sovereign cannot be a father—or else the father must be the very person of the nothing (nothing or "no one" ["*personne*"] is the same "thing").[11]

At this point the perspective is reversed: the "person of the nothing" (who cannot then be either a pure nothingness or "no one") or the "nonsubjective agency" (which nevertheless cannot be an object). This is what outlines exactly, around a hollow, the contours of sovereignty. To separate politics from sovereignty poses a problem, a problem whose schema is that of an antisovereignty, of a negative sovereignty, of a sovereignty without sovereignty: in sum, the schema of sovereignty itself, or the schema of the "very high" without altitude nor vantage point.

It is not sufficient, indeed, to designate politics as a regulatory organ of justice and of equality between the unequal and heterogeneous spheres of common existence (accepting that "common existence" is a pleonasm). It is still necessary that this vanishing line, or infinite perspective ("justice and equality"), trace a recognizable figure, not as a face but as a tracing of meaning. How can there be a meaning that is transversal or transcendent to all spheres of meaning, a truth of all meanings, in sum, and which, nevertheless, does not assume a subject, a substance, or, in the end, a Truth? The creation of such a meaning—the constituting, instituting, legislating gesture, a gesture that is always both foundational and revolutionary—is the proper concern of sovereignty. It is the concern, therefore, of that which carries in itself, of necessity, its own emptying.

Post-Scriptum

From what precedes, it must follow that instituting sovereignty cannot be itself instituted. Better still, there is not, in a general way, an instituted sovereignty: *contradictio in adjecto.* The summit bases itself as much as it "summits itself." Sovereignty takes place in thought as thought. Hegel understood this by writing that only philosophy contemplates the majesty of the sovereign.[12] That means that the exercise of sovereignty is the exercise of thought, at least if thought is understood as the act of reason in its most ontological and nongnosological sense (reason as *ratio*, a measure of the immeasurable summit). Precisely when the sovereign was a king, royalty had to be thought as such in order to be royal (thought: symbolized, represented, experienced, honored, and this to the heart of its being-nothing). The decapitation of the king signifies the laying bare of the thought of sovereignty: its message proclaimed in all the heads. This implies that its exercise is the same exercise of that which we call "citizenship" or "politics." Quite plainly, it cannot make philosophers, as specialists of a kind of discourse, into exceptional citizens: that means, on the contrary, that political thinking in act, or the political act, that is, the thinking act, is at stake in the actual actions of all citizens, and of everyone, and that everyone must have access to the conditions of this thought in act. But that refers necessarily also to the unique proximity of philosophers with politics, from Plato to Hegel, to Marx, and to Heidegger himself: this proximity defines the indistinct zone where knowledge can will itself all powerful but where, in a symmetrical manner, the sovereign power addresses its own thinking to itself.

P.-S. 2

The apolitical form of contemporary politics (the passage to the limit of the State) has already been named "Empire" several times (just as imperialism has been linked to the development of capitalism, and not only in the contemporary age but ever since the precapitalism of Antiquity). Empire does not pertain to sovereignty: it pertains to domination. The master is not the sovereign. The sovereign does not legitimize itself: it imposes itself in the name of a right that is already given and posited (the right of the *pater familias*, the right of the mighty, dynastic right, right of conquest). Sovereignty, if it must be thought, must be contrasted with empire. That is to say, precisely where the right is not given, a situation that perhaps properly defines right: what remains right as a fact, relation to a given fact as making right. Sovereignty supposes a fundamental contestation of any right acquired in this manner. Force cannot make right: this is Rousseau's axiom of which we are all persuaded, but which implies that the proper force of right poses a particular problem. The "reverse of empire" does not designate the project of a destruction of the Empire as was the case in the past for the destruction of the State (assuming that we have entered into an era of Empire) but the necessity of thinking both one and the other: that which could be proper to the form "Empire" while the form "Sovereign state" does not admit the reverse.[13]

P.-S. 3

A fragment. On the one hand the sovereignty of the State, as State, dislocates and fragments itself—without so much as impregnating the whole, contrary to the totalitarian desire. In this sense it is broken, decomposed, and does not know how to grasp the idea, nor the resource of its own instituting force. On the other hand, the same process shows that sovereignty, in its essence as *summit* is necessarily detached as extremity and as point that is incommensurable to a base and to an edifice. In fact, the summit cannot be connected to the edifice. In this sense sovereignty is a fragment in a more essential manner: it is a fragment that is not totalized on itself, a fragment in principled subtraction, a principle of subtraction and not imposition or foundation. In this respect, it is certain that sovereignty concerns the exception to which Carl Schmitt links it by definition. But it is a question precisely of thinking the exception: it is not only what gives itself outside of right, outside of the institution. It is also what does not give itself at all: that which is not a brute fact, a given that prevents a passage to the limit of right, but that withdraws from any given. It could be said that the exception exempts itself. The difficulty with Schmitt is perhaps that he sutures in silence this exemption of the exception, or the proper logic of the absence of foundation (and as we know, he was able to retrieve that operation with the name of "*der Führer*").

P.-S. 4

And if sovereignty was the revolt of the people?

3

Cosmos Basileus

The unity of a world is not one: it is made of a diversity, including disparity and opposition.[14] It is made of it, which is to say that it is not added it to it and does not reduce it. The unity of a world is nothing other than its diversity, and its diversity is, in turn, a diversity of worlds. A world is a multiplicity of worlds, the world is a multiplicity of worlds, and its unity is the sharing out [*partage*] and the mutual exposure in this world of all its worlds.

The sharing out of the world is the law of the world. The world does not have any other law, it is not submitted to any authority, it does not have any sovereign. *Cosmos/Nomos*. Its supreme law is in it as the multiple and mobile line of the sharing out that it is. *Nomos* is the distribution, the repartition, and the attribution of the parts. Territorial place, nourishment, a delimitation of rights and duties: to each and each time as appropriate.

But appropriate in what sense? The determination of appropriateness—the law of the law, absolute justice—is nowhere but in the sharing itself and in the exceptional singularity of each, of each case, according to this sharing. In any case, this sharing is not given, and "each" is not given (that which is the unity of each part, the occurrence of its case, the configuration of each world). It is not an accomplished distribution. The world is not given. It is itself the gift. The world is its own creation (this is what "creation" means). Its sharing is at every moment put into play: universe in expansion, illimitation of individuals, and infinite demand of justice. This is why, for us, *cosmos basileus* replaces Pindar's *nomos basileus*, the kingdom of a given law.

"Justice" designates what must be *rendered* (as one says in French, *rendre justice*). Justice must be restituted, returned, given in return to each singular existent: that which must be accorded to it in return of the gift that it itself is. And that entails also that we do not know exactly (one does not know *au juste* as, again, one says in French) who or what is a "singular existent," neither whence nor whither. By virtue of the gift and the incessant sharing of the world one does not know where the sharing of a stone or of a person begins or ends. The delineation is always wider and the same time more narrow than one believes when one grasps it (or rather one grasps quite well, as long as one is attentive to what extent the contour is trembling mobile and fleeting). Each existent belongs to more groups, masses, networks, or complexes than one first recognizes, and each also detaches from them and from itself, infinitely. Each opens and closes on more worlds and in it, as outside of it, hollowing out the outside inside and reciprocally.

What is appropriate is thus defined by the measure proper to each existent *and* to the infinite, indefinitely open, circulating and transforming community (or communication, contagion, contact) of all existences between them.

This is not a twofold appropriateness. It is the same, for community is not added to the existent. The existent does not have its own consistency and subsistence by itself: but it has it as the sharing of community. Community (which also has nothing subsistent by itself, which is contact, juxtaposition, porosity, osmosis, frictions, attraction and repulsion, etc.) is cosubstantial with the existent: to each and to all, to each as to all, to each insofar as all. This is, to translate in a certain language, the "mystical body" of the world, or in another language, the reciprocal action of the parts of the world. But in all the cases, it is coexistence by which existence itself and a world in general are defined.

Coexistence remains at an equal distance between juxtaposition and integration. Coexistence does not happen to existence from without, it does not add itself to it and one cannot subtract it from it: it is existence.

Existence is not made alone, if one can say it that way. It is *Being* that is alone, at least in all of the ordinary senses that one can give to being. But existence is nothing other than being exposed: expulsed from its simple self-identity and from its pure position, exposed to the event, to creation, thus to the outside, to exteriority, to multiplicity, to alterity, and to alteration. (In a sense, certainly, this is nothing other than being exposed to being itself, to its own "being" and also, consequently, being exposed as being: exposition as the essence of being.)

Justice is thus the return to each existent its due according to its unique creation, singular in its coexistence with all other creations. The two measures are not separate: the singular property exists according to the singular line that joins it to the other properties. What distinguishes is also what connects "with" and "together."

Justice must be rendered to the line of the proper, to its cut each time appropriate—a cut that does not cut and that does not rise from a background, but a common cut that in one stroke separates and makes contact, a coexistence whose indefinite intertwining is the sole ground on which the "form" of existence rises. There is then no ground: there is only the "with," proximity and its spacing, the strange familiarity of all the worlds in the world.

For each its most appropriate horizon is also its proximity with the other horizon: that of the coexistent, of all the coexistents, of coexisting totality. But "proximity" is not strong enough if one does not understand that all the horizons are the sides of the same cut, of the same sinuous and instantaneous line that is that of the world (its unity). This line is not proper to any existent, and even less to an other kind of substance that would loom over the world: it is the common impropriety, the non belonging and the non dependence, the absolute errancy of the creation of the world.

Justice must therefore be rendered both to the singular absoluteness of the proper and to the absolute impropriety of the community of existents. It must be rendered the same to each: such is the play (or the sense) of the world.

This is an infinite justice, consequently, which must be rendered both to the propriety of each and the impropriety common to all: rendered to birth and to death, which hold between them the infinity of meaning. Or rather: it must be rendered to birth and to death, which are, one with the other and one into the other (or one through the other), the infinite overflowing of meaning, and therefore of justice. This is a birth and death about which it is appropriate—this is the strict justice of truth—to say nothing, but about which true speech desperately seeks the proper words.

This infinite justice is visible nowhere. On the contrary, an unbearable injustice is unleashed everywhere: the earth trembles, the viruses infect, men are criminals, liars, and executioners.

Justice cannot be removed from the mire or fog of injustice, any more than it can be projected as a supreme conversion of injustice. It is intrinsic to infinite justice that it must collide brutally with injustice. But how and why it is intrinsic to it, one cannot explain. This no longer pertains to interrogations on reason or pertains to the demands of meaning. It is intrinsic to the infinity of justice and to the uninterrupted creation of the world: in such a way that infinity is never in any way called to accomplish itself, not even (above all) as an infinite return of self into self. Birth and death, sharing and coexistence belong to the infinite. The infinite, as it were, appears and disappears, divides itself and coexists: it is the movement, the agitation of the general diversity of the worlds, which make the world (and which "unmake" it as well).

This is why justice is always also—and perhaps first—the demand for justice: the complaint and protestation against injustice, the call that cries out for justice, and the breath that exhausts itself for it. The law of justice is this unappeasable tension toward justice itself. Similarly, the law of the world is an infinite tension toward the world itself. These two laws are not only homologous; they are the same and unique law of absolute sharing (one could say: the law of the Absolute as sharing.)

Justice does not come from the outside (what outside?) to hover above the world, to repair or accomplish it. It is given with the world, in it and as the very law of its givenness. There is no sovereign, no temple nor tablet of the law, which is not strictly speaking the world itself, the severe, inextricable, and unachievable line of its horizon. One could be tempted to say: there is a justice for the world, and there is a world for justice. But these finalities or these reciprocal intentions will express what is at stake very poorly. The world is to itself the supreme law of its justice: not the given world "such as it is," but rather the fact that the world happens, a properly incongruent congruence. The only task of justice is thus to create a world tirelessly, the space of an unappeasable and always unsettled sovereignty of meaning.

Notes

Translators' Introduction

1. Jean-Luc Nancy, *The Creation of the World* or *Globalization*, trans. François Raffoul and David Pettigrew (Albany: State University of New York Press, 2007). Hereafter cited as CW, followed by the page number.

2. Following the proposed alternative by Nancy: "can what is called 'globalization' give rise to a world, or to its contrary?" (CW, 29).

3. Nancy will add in a note farther in the text that the term *globalization* could just as easily be referred to as "agglomerization" (CW, 118, n.5), in reference to the *glomus*. As for the concept of the "bad infinite," which Nancy borrows from Hegel, it signifies in this context that the infinite "is indeed the one that cannot be *actual*" (CW, 39), that is, the bad infinite "of a 'globalization' in spiral" (CW, 47), which Nancy contrasts with the actual infinite of the finite being (CW, 71). Let us simply indicate that the infinite in action signifies for Nancy the world itself as "absolute value," that is to say, as the existence of the world put into play as "absolute existence" (CW, 44) so much so that it is necessary "in the end, that the world has absolute value for itself" (CW, 40).

4. Nancy evokes on several occasions globalization as an event that "sweeps" over us, which comes to us from an unspeakable elsewhere, and which, through a weakening of "independencies and sovereignties" and of "representations of belonging" that makes itself (CW, 37), opening the possibility of a questioning of the proper and of identity. The world as such gives itself to vision in this weakening, because it is nothing other than the putting-into-play of a possible habitation.

5. He writes, for example, "the future is precisely what exceeds representation. And we have learned that it is a matter for us of reconceiving the world outside of representation" (CW, 50).

6. Nancy also clarifies: "At the end of monotheism, there is the world without God, *that is to say, without another world*" (CW, 50; our emphasis).

113

7. Jean-Luc Nancy. *The Sense of the World*, trans. Jeffrey Librett (Minneapolis: University of Minnesota Press, 1997). Henceforth cited as SW followed by the page number.

8. Nancy thus will specify that the world is a dimensionality without origin, founded on nothing, an "archi-spatiality" or a "spaciousness of the opening" without a provenance of being but that is a "spacing of presences" (always plural and singular) (CW, 73).

9. On the difference between sense and signification, see the opening pages of *The Sense of the World*.

10. The decisive characteristic of the becoming-world of the world, explains Nancy, "is the feature through which the world resolutely and absolutely distances itself from any status as object in order to tend toward being itself the 'subject' of its own 'worldhood'—or 'world-forming.' But being a subject in general means having to become oneself" (CW, 41).

11. On poverty, see the recent edition and translation by Philippe Lacoue-Labarthe and Ana Samardzija of the Heidegger lecture on June 27, 1945, *La pauvreté [Die Armut]* (Strasbourg: Presses universitaires de Strasbourg, 2004).

12. In the following chapter, "Of Creation," Nancy will analyze the expression "to come to the world": "That 'coming to the world' means birth and death, emerging from nothing and going to nothing" (CW, 74).

13. "If 'creation' means anything, it is the exact opposite of any form of production in the sense of a fabrication which supposes a given, a project, and a producer. The idea of creation, such as it has been elaborated in the most diverse and most convergent thoughts . . . above all means the idea of the *ex nihilo*" (CW, 51).

14. "The 'nothing' of creation is what opens in God when God withdraws in it (and in sum *from* it) in the act of creating. God annihilates itself [*s'anéantit*] as a "self" or as a distinct being in order to "withdraw" in its act—which makes the opening of the world" (CW, 70). Also, a few lines farther: "The unique God, whose unicity is the correlate of the creating act, cannot precede its creation, any more that it can subsist above it or apart from it in some way. It merges with it: merging with it, it withdraws in it and withdrawing there it empties itself there, emptying itself it is nothing other than the opening of this void. Only the opening is divine, but the divine is nothing more than the opening" (ibid.).

15. However, it is important to stress that Nancy refuses to simply oppose two different fates of the world as if they represented different levels of existence. This is the sense of the "ex" just mentioned. As he explains in his reading of Marx, "Extortion or the exposure of each through the others [*exposition des uns par les autres*]: the most important is not to say, 'here is the decisive alternative!' (which we already know). What matters is to be able to think how this proximity of the two 'ex-' or this twofold excess is produced, *how the same world is divided in this way.* (CW, 46; our emphasis). Also, "What is most troubling about the modern enigma—for specifically this is what constitutes the modern and which makes it, for the last three centuries, an enigma for itself, which even

defines the modern as such an enigma, without any need to speak of the "postmodern"—is that the without-reason could take the form both of capital and of the mystical rose which represents the absolute value of the "without-reason" (CW, 50).

16. Nancy explains that, "Philosophy begins from itself: this is a permanent axiom for it, which is implicit or explicit in the work of all philosophers" (CW, 77).

17. The movement of history is in and of itself the withdrawal of nature and naturality. Nancy thus explains that "[h]istory is not 'nature,' if 'nature' has its origin and end in itself (supposing that nature exists or rather that it *still* exists in a *history* which precisely locates elsewhere, without end, the very naturality of any nature: as if that history included henceforth the *natura naturans* of any *natura naturata* and, consequently also its *natura denaturans*.) History is the infinite deferral of any nature and this is why, from now on, the following question occurs to us: was there ever 'nature,' since there was history, and thus an indefinite deferral of any nature?" (CW, 79).

18. "With the becoming human," he explains, "this movement appears to itself as its own principle and its own end. That is to say, properly without principle and without end since it proceeds from an initial detachment, which one can name 'human condition' and whose permanence involves an extreme instability and mutability of what has thus been detached (contingency forms thus the necessity of this 'history'). And that is what we can call, feigning to believe that there would have been first a pure and stable 'nature': *denaturation*. And one could then say that 'humanity' is the indexical name of the indefinite and infinite term of the human denaturation" (CW, 87).

19. For instance, with respect to what we might call the *aporia* of the subject, Nancy shows how, in the self-inauguration of philosophy, the subject that philosophy "wants to be, of this inauguration, undoes itself or destitutes itself . . . in the very gesture of its inauguration"(CW, 83).

20. Nancy explains that "our expectation of the future is henceforth deprived of anticipation, of representation, and of concept"(CW, 82).

21. *Der Ister.* A film by David Barison and Daniel Ross, 2004.

22. Michel Foucault, *History of Sexuality Volume I: An Introduction*, trans. Robert Hurley (New York: Vintage Books, 1980). Henceforth cited as HS followed by the page number.

23. It would in fact be more a matter of an "ecotechnology" insofar as natural life has become indissociable from a series of technological conditions. Farther on, he would clarify his reservations with respect to the motif of life, explaining that life is an "insufficient" notion to designate the managed, regulated, or deregulated totality intended in the notion of bio-politics, and that "'world' would be a more precise notion: a 'world' as the reverse of a 'cosmos,' and as concern (mourning and awaiting) for a 'totality of meaning'" (CW, 125, n.13).

24. This problematic is reminiscent of Foucault's treatment in *Technologies of the Self* of "technologies of power" and of "technologies of self." In this seminar, Foucault speaks of these two technologies in particular as "technologies of domination" (TS, 18).

25. For instance, Nancy insists that politics cannot be thought in terms of subjectivity. Rather, it would be a matter of showing how sovereignty "no longer designates the assumption of a subject or in a subject," but instead, "the order of the subjectless regulation of the relation between subjects." On this between, farther on he evokes the "empty space of sovereignty," itself to be understood as the nonsubstantial between of sharing, a sovereignty structured in that sharing of the world (CW, 104).

26. In *The Inoperative Community*, trans. Peter Connor, Lisa Garbus, Michael Holland, and Simona Sawhney (Minneapolis: University of Minnesota Press, 1991), henceforth cited as IC followed by the page number, Nancy cites Bataille's comment that "Sovereignty is NOTHING." Sovereignty is an exposure to an excess, a transcendence. Nancy emphasizes that such an excess "does not present itself and does not let itself be appropriated (or simulated)" (IC, 18). Nancy speaks of the limits of Bataille's thought, a thought that was perhaps trapped in a circle between communism and fascism. Nancy seeks to conceive of sovereignty in terms of singular existences. These singular existences are sovereign in their difference; a sovereign difference that is shared. Nancy addresses the work of George Bataille as a forerunner to the thinking of a community that exists in a destabilizing excess of itself. Such a community would exceed totalization. In the *Inoperative Community*, Nancy credits Bataille with being the first to experience the inability to regain any immanence in the "outside of itself" of a lost communion (IC, 9). Such a community communicates ecstasis. However, Nancy is circumspect about Bataille's thinking with respect to the poles of community (communism) and ecstasis (fascism). He writes that Bataille "gave up the task of thinking community properly speaking" (IC, 25).

27. Giorgio Agamben, *Homo Sacer: Sovereign Power and Bare Life*, trans. Daniel Heller-Roazen (Stanford: Stanford University Press, 1998) and *State of Exception*, trans. Kevin Attell (Chicago: University of Chicago Press, 2005).

28. Carl Schmitt, *Political Theology: Four Chapters on the Concept of Sovereignty*, trans. George Schwab (Cambridge: The MIT Press, 1985), 1. On page 2 of the same text, Schmitt continues, "The decision on the exception is a decision in the true sense of the word." Schmitt's point is that the sovereign is the sovereign only insofar as it makes this decision. Without this power, there is no real power. Henceforth cited as PT followed by the page number.

29. Carl Schmitt, *The Concept of the Political*, trans. George Schwab (Chicago: University of Chicago Press, 1996), 36. Henceforth cited as CP followed by the page number.

30. Carl Schmitt, *Legality and Legitimacy*, trans. Jeffrey Seitzer (Durham: Duke University Press, 2004), 35. Henceforth cited as LL followed by the page number.

31. Hajo Holburn, *A History of Modern Germany. 1840–1945* (New York: Knopf, 1969), p. 724.

32. Hardt and Negri speak in *Empire* of a "control that extends throughout the depths of the consciousnesses and bodies of the population—and at the same time across

the entirety of social relations," and Agamben specifies that the state of exception has become "the dominant paradigm of government in contemporary politics" (SE, 2).

33. Jacques Derrida, "The Force of Law," in *Deconstruction and the Possibility of Justice*, ed. D. Cornell, M. Rosenfeld, and D. Carlson (New York: Routledge, 1992), 30. Henceforth cited as FL followed by the page number.

34. On page 35 of SE, Agamben asserts that Carl Schmitt's theory of sovereignty depends first on his notion of the state of exception. There is for Nancy as well a primacy of the state of exception from which the singular plural existences create the world.

Author's Prefatory Note to the English Language Edition

1. TN. We have chosen to render *mondialisation* (which in French is the word used for what the English-speaking world knows as *globalization*) as "world-forming," in order to maintain the reference to "world" that Nancy seeks to emphasize in contrast to "global," as well as in order to retain the sense of a creation of meaning that is inherent in Nancy's notion of world. Hence the term *world-forming* will contrast with globalization following Nancy's intention in this book.

Urbi et Orbi

A first version of this text was written for a lecture given in Bordeaux, in March 2001, in the context of the cultural event "Mutations" organized by the association Arc-en-rêve and by Nadia Tazzi.

1. Georg Wilhelm Friedrich Hegel, "Relationship of Skepticism to Philosophy, Exposition of Its Different Modifications and Comparison to the Latest Form with the Ancient One," in *Between Kant and Hegel. Texts in the Development of Post-Kantian Idealism*, ed. and trans. George di Giovanni and H. S. Harris (Albany: State University of New York Press, 1985), 333.

2. TN. The term *immonde* is used ordinarily in French to mean "base," "vile," or "foul," but Nancy plays here with the literal sense of the term, which we have kept and rendered accordingly as un-world.

3. TN. Nancy plays here on the term "*capital(e)*": capital as monetary concept and capital as a city.

4. Karl Marx, *The German Ideology*, in *The Marx-Engels Reader*, ed. Robert C. Tucker (New York: W. W. Norton, 1978), 163–64. Henceforth cited as MER followed by the page number. Translation slightly modified. (The German term translated by "creation" is indeed its corresponding *Schöpfung*: one could study in Marx the usages of this term and its relation with value in itself, that is to say, with work in itself, as well as its difference and its relation with the *Produktion* that pertains to the interdependency of work.)

5. "Globalization" is the term that is most generally used outside of France. Its critical sense could also be rendered, following what I have indicated with respect to *glomus*, by *agglomerization* [*agglomérisation*] . . .

6. This also means that "Marx has not yet been received," as Derrida says in *Specters of Marx: The State of the Debt, The Work of Mourning, and the New International*, trans. Peggy Kamuf (New York: Routledge, 1994), 174. A minimally rigorous reading of Marx, whether from Derrida or another (Michel Henry for instance, or Etienne Balibar, or André Tosel, or Jacques Bidet, among others), confirms this observation. But we must add two remarks: on the one hand, doesn't the history of the world today, under the guise of "globalization," produce as its own necessity the scheme of an entirely different "reception" of Marx, and, on the other hand, isn't the fact of not yet being received and never being completely received, the reason that the force of a thought goes beyond itself and its proper name?

7. The clearest text is perhaps that of "Marginal Notes on Adolphe Wagner's '*Lehrbuch der politischen Ökonomie*,'" in Vol. 24 in *The Collected Works of Karl Marx and Frederick Engels*, 50 volumes (New York: International Publishers, London: Lawrence and Wishart Ltd., 1975–), 531 and particularly the section "Derivation of the Concept of Value."

8. "Mysterious" and "mystical," are words that Marx uses with respect to fetishism. Cf. *Capital*, I, I section, 4. MER, 319–20.

9. No doubt the problem does not end there, any more than the more general question of phenomenality. The nonphenomenal and yet actual presence remains a motif to explore. But I cannot dwell on it here.

10. This is, clearly, a provisional image. But it is a matter of at least indicating that the reality of value is not simply economic, or, in a more complex way, that the reality of economy is not economic in the simple mercantile sense, perhaps even that the reality of the market is not . . . , etc. In any case, the reality of the phenomenon is no more here than elsewhere identifiable as a "pure phenomenon." On this "phenomenological" complexity and its implications in the relation "use-value–exchange-value," I refer the reader to Jacques Derrida, *Specters of Marx*, chapter 5, "apparition of the inapparent: the phenomenological 'conjuring trick,'" particularly p. 160: "[O]ne would have to say that the phantasmagoria began before the said exchange-value, at the threshold of the value of value in general. . . ." On the reality of the economy one can reread Michel Henry, *Marx: A Philosophy of Human Reality*, trans. Kathleen McLaughlin (Bloomington: Indiana University Press, 1983), chapter 7, "The Reality of Economic Reality" (even if to disagree with his interpretation of "living reality"); as for the reality of the relation of "expression" in which value is constituted and on the nature of "concept" or the "content of thought," one can look up the work by Pierre Macherey ("*A propos du processus d'exposition du 'Capital'*"), in *Lire le Capital* (PUF, Paris 1996). At the intersection between these diverse approaches, one will find at least one common point: the character of a value "in itself," which precisely is not a "thing in itself" but the actuality of a *praxis* that has "value" by itself absolutely and in the materiality or the complex corpo-

reality of the transformation in which it expresses itself, gives itself, and creates itself. Reconsidering here the famed "epistemological break" of Althusser, I am wondering if one should not understand, under the guise of "epistemology" that was then in usage, that it was not a matter of elaborating anew, against an idealism of value, a *practical* thought of value, which first meant: against a humanism that presupposed "human value," a thought presupposing the insufficiency of the concept of "man" faced with the absolute value of a "creation of man." See Louis Althusser, "Marxism and Humanism," in *For Marx*, trans. Ben Brewster (New York: Verso, 1990).

11. No doubt it is possible, and perhaps necessary, to understand "value" in Marx according to what Louis Gernet explains of the "The Mythical Idea of Value in Greece," in *The Anthropology of Ancient Greece*, trans. John Hamilton SJ, and Blaise Nagy (Baltimore: Johns Hopkins University Press, 1981), on the condition that we understand well that "mythical" designates here the reality of the "virtue of symbols" (178). Namely: the value of the valorous ones who measure themselves in the athletic *agón*, recompensed by a "prize" the material reality of which, a "pricey" object, does not have "value" as a monetary currency would, but as an offering (royal and divine) given to the one who shows his or her worth as the most valorous: wealth here is not capitalized (that would be *hubris*) but it makes the brilliance of what "shows its worth" shine in gold, which we might risk translating into a "to produce oneself"—produce what? Nothing other than a valorous man, or the value of a man. But this happens, Gernet tells us, before the invention of currency, and competition does not yield to commerce, if we can say it in this way. However, Gernet does note that continuities are maintained between "mythical value" and "monetary value," and we know that on this point much could be added (in particular from psychoanalysis). How can we articulate with precision the relation I am sketching here between Marx and the "mythical" world, between abstract value and symbolic value (in the strong, active and ostensive sense of the word)? This is what needs to be elaborated.

12. As we can understand, this remark means that Heidegger's concern with respect to humanism hardly differs from Marx's with reference to "total man."

13. Georg Wilhelm Friedrich Hegel, *The Encyclopedia of Philosophical Sciences*, trans. Gustav Emil Mueller (New York: Philosophical Library, 1959), §94, 125. The "good" infinite, infinite *in act*, is that which is identical to the finite in which it actualizes itself.

14. One will find numerous indications in Paul Clavier's *Le concept de monde* (Paris: PUF, 2000), a perspective however quite different from mine.

15. TN. Nancy plays on the polysemy of the word *sens*, which includes: meaning, direction, and in this particular case function or even usage.

16. See the final page of Martin Heidegger, "The Age of the World Picture," in *The Question Concerning Technology and Other Essays*, trans. William Lovitt (New York: Harper, 1977), 153.

17. With respect to "secularization" and to the necessity of opposing to that model the model-less thought of another (il)legitimation of the modern world, I can only

refer to Hans Blumenberg, who seems to me to be the unavoidable point of departure in this matter.

18. On this question, see Jean-Luc Nancy, *L' "il y a" du rapport sexuel* (Paris: Galilée, 2001).

19. See supra, p. 119, n.11, relative to the "mythical value" analysed by Gernet. Let us clarify the following: it does not matter whether the archeo-philological deduction of such an operation be exact or not, from the perspective of empirical knowledge. One cannot moreover ignore that phenomena of precapitalization have preceded capitalism, nor in general that wealth as power has always accompanied wealth as brilliance, just as religion as domination has always accompanied sacred symbolism. What matters is that capitalism forces us to seek the value of value, whose extensive form it deploys so exactly that it renders all the more insistent its absence of intensive form (an absence that we interpret as a loss, which remains certainly insufficient, as would any thought of loss). Capitalism exposes the inverted form of an absolute and singular value through general equivalence. What can the reversal of this inversion, or "revolution," mean in Marx's terms?

20. I will limit myself to mentioning here, Martin Heidegger, *The Principle of Reason*, trans. Reginald Lilly (Bloomington: Indiana University Press, 1991). In reality, it is a matter of commenting upon, or better, of extending and taking farther that thought according to which the "principle of sufficient reason" becomes an imperious demand of reason when it becomes sensible, if not intelligible, that neither reason nor ground sustains the world.

21. This was the sense of the word in French, and the German kept the two senses of *reich/Reich*. One can note an analogous displacement of the sense of *fortune*.

22. In German, it is still this *Würde*, which one translates by "dignity" (in Kant, for instance), but which belongs to the semantic group of *Wert*, "value."

23. "*Absentheism*": an absent God and an absence in place of God, but also the absence from work as liberation from servitude or as the sabbatical rest of the creating God (Genesis II: 2–3), the rest of the one who nevertheless does not know fatigue (*Koran* L, 38), vacancy of the vacant . . . (One also called the landowners who never appear on their land "absentheists"!)

24. Ludwig Wittgenstein, *Tractatus Logico-Philosophicus*, trans. D. F. Pears and B. F. McGuinness (New York: Routledge, 2001), 6.41, 86. Henceforth cited as TLP followed by the page number.

25. In the sense that a world is itself a space of meaning, see Jean-Luc Nancy, *The Sense of the World*.

26. This is the moment to note many analogies or places of encounter between this work and the work of Antonio Negri in *Kairos, Alma Venus, multitude*, trans. Judith Revel (Paris: Calmann-Lévy, 2001), a book that I was only able to read after this text was

already written. In particular, the motif of creation plays an important role in Negri (although he does not refer to its theological provenance, nonetheless apparent). But if there is more than one disagreement, the point where I am most in disagreement with him is the following: for him, "meaning" seems to be posited as something obvious, and its nature not questioned. It seems to me, on the contrary, that everything here requires that we rethink the meaning of meaning, including as common sense (or sense of the common), or rather as such. But if meaning is always of the common and in common, it does not follow that the "common" makes immediate sense: it has to produce itself (thus think itself) as such—as "meaning-in-common," which means forms, languages, arts, celebrations, philosophies, etc. One must therefore think the *works* in which meaning creates itself in a determined way, even if its creation largely exceeds the closed space of the works. And we must think how these works communicate meaning—which is not "their" meaning.

Of Creation

1. *La Faculté de juger* (collectif), (Paris: Minuit, 1985).

2. Jean-François Lyotard, *The Confession of Augustine*, trans. Richard Beardsworth (Stanford: Stanford University Press, 2000), 37.

3. Jean-François Lyotard, *Libidinal Economy*, trans. Iain Hamilton Grant (Bloomington: Indiana University Press, 1993), 255.

4. Jean-François Lyotard, *Lessons on the Analytic of the Sublime*, trans. Elizabeth Rottenberg (Stanford: Stanford University Press, 1994), 114.

5. Richard McKeon, ed., Aristotle, *Metaphysics*, Δ, 2, 1013 b 25, in *The Basic Works of Aristotle* (New York: Random House, 1941), 753.

6. Immanuel Kant, *The Critique of Judgment*, trans, James Meredith Creed (Oxford: Clarendon Press, 1982), ¶ 65, 19–24

7. Richard McKeon, ed. *Metaphysics*, Z, 17, 1041 a 10–25, in *The Basic Works of Aristotle* (New York: Random House, 1941), 810.

8. Immanuel Kant, *Critique of Pure Reason*, trans. Norman Kemp Smith (New York: St. Martin's Press, 1965), 210.

9. Ibid., 215.

10. In this respect, Spinoza represents, ahead of his time, a conjunction of this "possible" and of the "real," a way of gathering the "giving" and the "doing," which moreover suppresses at the same time the difficulties and aporias linked to a "God" and to a "creation," a creation that Kant analyzed and critiqued. This is why one saw, following Kant, a flurry of Spinozisms. However, the Spinozist's substance still keeps at a distance, or neutralizes, it seems to me, the question of the "generosity" of the world as I wish to indicate it here (more than one Spinozist, I know, will disagree with me . . .).

11. It is important to mention briefly that it is precisely this status of the image of the creator (status of man but also in some respect of the universe and/or nature) that will have made possible, or even necessary, the transformation we are speaking of here. In other words, this transformation comes from the fact that creation is not first production (we will get to this later) but expression, exposition, or *extraneation* of "itself." With Leibniz, it consists in the "continual outflashings of the divinity." Gottfried Wilhelm Leibniz, *Monadology*, in *Leibniz: Discourse on Metaphysics, Corrrespondence with Arnauld, Monadology*, trans. George Montgomery (La Salle, IL: Open Court, 1980), ¶ 47, 261.

12. This is also the reason why it is possible and desirable to show that the Kantian revolution in its entirety rests on nothing other than a question of creation, at the same time recognized and rejected by Kant himself (the great book by Gehrard Krüger on Kant's morals includes more than an indication on this issue).

13. We recognize here a corollary of Kant's thesis on being, which "is not a real predicate." Not being a predicate, *being* is the *subject* of existence and as such it "is" *nothing* other than existence.

14. Of which it is a common feature quite independent from their well-known differences.

15. All the necessary arguments are in particular present and often repeated by Valery (see his *Cahiers, passim*).

16. But also in more than one spiritual meditation, neither properly mystical nor properly speculative, such as that of Simone Weil, to give a modern example.

17. See "*La déconstruction du christianisme*," a very succinct sketch of this theme published in *Etudes philosophiques* 2 (1998), and the indications already given in *Being Singular Plural*, trans. Robert Richardson and Anne O'Byrne (Stanford: Stanford University Press, 2000), and then in *La Pensée dérobée* (Paris: Galilée, 2001).

18. As Heidegger invites us to think in *What is Philosophy*, trans. William Kluback and Jean T. Wilde (Albany: NCUP Inc., 1956). Being is not simply an intransitive verb: it speaks intransitivity itself, but it speaks it in such a way that it must be heard in "the transitive sense" (49).

19. I will reserve a precise examination of the philological and theological history of the vocabulary of creation for another occasion. Let us recall here that the mystical rose (see above page 47) *grows* [croît] without reason.

20. A displacement of the thought of desire also results from this: see *L' "il y a" du rapport sexuel*.

21. I will not address the references that would be necessary, with respect to the Kabbalah (in particular the studies from Gershom Scholem) as well as other interpretations, whether Christian or Muslim, of "creation," and I will not draw upon Schelling's analyses: all this, clearly, remains in the background.

22. Gérard Granel, *Etudes* (Paris: Galilée, 1995), 126 and 132.

23. Ludwig Wittgenstein, "A Lecture on Ethics," *The Philosophical Review* LXXIV, no. 1 (1965): 8.

24. Jean-Luc Marion, for his part, attempts to refer this difference to a "difference without compare [*sans égale*]" that would be prior [*en deçà*] to any temporality and in the simultaneity of a "call" and a "responsal." Jean-Luc Marion, *Being Given: Toward a Phenomenology of Givenness*, trans. Jeffrey L. Kosky (Stanford: Stanford University Press, 2002), 295. This powerful and eloquent proposition does not emerge yet out of a "self-giving" (and of a "self-showing") of the phenomenon, whereas I propose here, simply, that *nothing* gives *itself* and that *nothing* shows *itself*—and that is what is.

25. The aporia of the gift, according to Derrida, is that it "must not even be what it has to be, namely, a gift" (*Given Time: Counterfeit Money*, trans. Peggy Kamuf [Chicago: University of Chicago Press, 1992], 69), since it cannot wish to give nor will itself as gift without suppressing its own generosity and gratuity. The gift is nothing, or gives nothing. This is the sense that one must give to the "this is nothing" that a giver says after he/she is thanked.

26. Contemporary astrophysics and cosmology do not cease, in this respect, to nourish thought and questioning.

27. Martin Heidegger, *Contributions to Philosophy (From Enowning)*, trans. Parvis Emad and Kenneth Maly (Bloomington: Indiana University Press, 1999), 61. We can recall that creation, in Babylonians myths where the monotheistic narrations find their sources, is first of all a separation, for instance of sky and earth, or of earth and water. To create is not to posit, but to separate.

Creation as Denaturation: Metaphysical Technology

This text, presented in Fribourg-en-Brisgau in 2000 at the Congress of the *Deutsche Gesellschaft für phänomenologische Forschung*, reconsiders and also revises selections of a presentation devoted to Alan Badiou's polemical relation to Heideggerian historicity (or historicality) and is forthcoming in the proceedings of the Colloquium devoted to Alain Badiou, "*La pensée forte*," organized in October 1999 in Bordeaux.

1. Martin Heidegger, *Nietzsche*, vol. II, trans. P. Klossowski (Paris: Gallimard, 1971), 381 (sec. ix "being").

2. On this word and its motif, this work recalls here (as well as through mutual textual communication) the work of Philippe Lacoue-Labarthe in *Poétique de l'histoire* (Paris: Galilée, 2002).

3. In truth it would be necessary to undertake a work specifically devoted to the way in which philosophy envisions or refuses to envision its own beginnings: from Plato to Heidegger it excludes the anthropological investigation of its provenance, and the self-engendering, whatever it is called (*logos* or *thaumazein*), institutes itself and reflects itself. It is as if philosophy had to be a second nature, rather than the technology of denatured truth ...

4. "Meaning" as question, tension, and intentionality, as passion too, and passion for truth, proceeds from the absence of given meaning, or what Bernard Stiegler called, "the originary disorientation" in *Technics and Time I: The Fault of Epimethus* (Stanford: Stanford University Press, 1998).

5. Serge Margel, *Logique de la nature* (Paris: Galilée, 2000).

6. Richard McKeon, ed., *Metaphysics* A, 982 b22, in *The Basic Works of Aristotle* (New York: Random House, 1941), 692.

Complements

1. The word *biopolitics* can also assume the following meaning today: "an ethico-socio-political reflection on the problems posed by biological technoscience," with an emphasis at times on "political power interested the biotechnological possibilities." . . . Thus to limit ourselves to a few recent examples in the volume *Biopolitik*, directed by Christian Geyer (Frankfurt-am-Main: Surkamp), as in no. 1 of *Multitudes*, "Biopolitique et Biopouvoir" (Exils, 2000), which opens discussions on the concept itself.

2. No doubt one also encounters more narrow usages of the word. But I consider here the usages that claim to be the most properly philosophical and to engage with this term propositions that fundamentally reevaluate each of the terms that compose it. I do not seek to classify these usages under names or works: I am only characterizing tendencies.

3. Human life was what was at issue for Foucault. We see without difficulty that vegetable and animal life followed a parallel destiny at the same time (breeding, care, etc). In any case, that destiny began long ago ever since the beginnings of cultivation and breeding. Certainly, there is henceforth a mutation in this technological continuum: the question is precisely of learning to understand it.

4. On the condition of not confusing, as is often the case, between "sovereignty" and "domination."

5. See below note 13 on page 125.

6. An early version of *Ex Nihilo Summum* was presented at a colloquium entitled "Sovereignty" at the Regional center of literature at Montpellier, Castries château, July 2001.

7. *Dictionnaire historique de l'ancien langage français: ou Glossaire de la langue française* (Paris: Niort, 1875–1882).

8. TN. See Jean Bodin, *On Sovereignty: Four Chapters From Six Books of the Commonwealth*, ed. and trans. Julian H. Franklin (Cambridge: Cambridge University Press, 1992).

9. TN. Jean-Jacques Rousseau, *The Social Contract*, trans. Maurice Cranston (London: Penguin Books, 1968).

10. TN. In English in the original.

11. TN. Nancy plays here on the twofold sense of the word *personne* in French, which means either person or no one.

12. Hegel, *Philosophy of Right* §281, trans. T. M. Knox (Oxford: Oxford University Press, 1967). "Hence the majesty of the monarch is a topic for thoughtful treatment by philosophy alone, since every method of inquiry, other than the speculative method of the infinite Idea which is purely self-grounded, annuls the nature of majesty altogether." (186)

13. This determination is similar to those that Michael Hardt and Antonio Negri suggest with their concept of "Empire": absence of borders, suspension of history, social integration [see Michael Hardt and Antonio Negri, *Empire* (Cambridge: Harvard University Press, 2001)]. In brief, it would be a question of a Moebius strip, each side of which passes incessantly into the other. That is not sufficient reason, to my mind, to make of this "Empire" "the *biopolitical* nature of the new paradigm of power" (E, 23), because power does not sets itself up there as such in the same way as in the State, and because "life" is a quite insufficient notion to designate such a managed regulated or deregulated totality. The "world" would be a more precise notion: a "world" as the reverse of a "cosmos," and as concern (mourning and awaiting) for a "totality of meaning."

14. TN. An earlier version of this essay appeared in *Being Singular Plural*. Professor Nancy has revised the text and a new translation has been provided of the entire essay.

Index